IT'S MAGIC

IT'S MAGIC

HENRY GORDON

Stoddart

First published in 1988 by
Stoddart Publishing Co. Limited
34 Lesmill Road
Toronto, Canada
M3B 2T6

Canadian Cataloguing in Publication Data

Gordon, Henry, 1919-
It's Magic

ISBN 0-7737-5149-1

1. Conjuring — Juvenile literature. I. Title.

GV1548.G67 1988 j793.8 C88-093080-2

ILLUSTRATIONS © 1988 Peter Grau
DESIGN: Brant Cowie / Art Plus
COVER PHOTOGRAPH: Peter Paterson

Printed in Canada

Contents

To Laura and Joey — two Magical personalities

Preface

Young readers of *THE TORONTO SUN-DAY STAR* usually turn to the *STARSHIP* page which is reserved for their age group. My column, *IT'S MAGIC*, has been appearing there for several years. This book contains a collection of many of these columns which I have selected for your enjoyment.

I must express my thanks to the *STAR-SHIP* editor, Agatha Bardoel, with whom I have worked since the column began. Agatha has certainly made sure that each trick is a practical one, and that it works. Which means that you, the reader, are holding a magic book which will be useful and, I hope, entertaining.

I have made sure that each effect follows certain rules. The materials used must be everyday articles which you can find around the home, or can purchase for a few cents. There are no magical props to buy.

There is no difficult sleight-of-hand to learn. The tricks are fairly simple and can be performed by any young person. And still, they are mystifying enough to fool many an adult.

Happy magishing.

Introduction

If you are a beginner in the field of magical conjuring I believe I know what you are going to do. You are going to skip this introduction and get right into the tricks which follow. Everyone wants to know the secrets. "How do the tricks work? I want to be a magician."

Well, I wouldn't recommend that you do this. How the tricks work is just part of the secrets of magic. The real secret is knowing how to present the tricks — how to act like a real magician, and to entertain your audience as well as mystify them.

So in this introduction I'm going to set down a few of the basic principles which I think you should learn, and always remember.

If you perform a trick, and do it well, you will usually fool the onlooker. But that alone is not "magic." That is just a puzzle. What you are really saying is I know the secret and you don't — which makes me smarter than you are.

Now, people don't like to be told they're not as smart as you are. But if your present your trick in an entertaining manner and make it seem really magical your audience will be amazed, amused, relaxed — and you will get the applause you deserve.

When you begin to perform magic you will probably feel very uneasy. Whenever you do a trick you will have the feeling that everyone knows how it was done. This is because very often the secret is quite simple, and, knowing it, you may feel that others can probably see or figure it out.

After a while you'll see that isn't so. This will give you more and more confidence, and you will realize that you are in charge. At that point remember two things. First, don't act like a know-it-all. It's important that your audience likes you as a performer. Second, always try to remember that your audience is just as bright as you are — sometimes brighter. So don't get careless in your presentation of the tricks.

By the way, I keep referring to "tricks." But that's just between you and me. I don't like using that word in front of an audience. After all, you're not trying to trick them — you're entertaining them with magic. So, instead of "trick", try using the words "miracle", "wonder", "effect", "experiment" or anything else that seems appropriate.

How do you know if, when you perform a trick, you have really fooled the spectators? There are two things they will usually ask after it is over. These questions are usually a giveaway that you've stunned them.

The first is, "How did you do that?" Which brings us to one of the most important things you must learn as a conjurer. Never, but never, reveal the secret of a trick. Please reread the last sentence and memorize it.

I have seen so many beginners make this mistake. They are so impressed by how clever the secret is, and so excited by having fooled the audience, that they can't wait to show how it was done.

What happens when you give away the secret? First of all, you are being unethical by not following the basic rule for all magicians: keep the secret. Secondly, when the spectator learns the secret, he or she is usually disappointed. What had looked like real magic, and stimulated the imagination, is now shown to be just a trick with a fairly simple secret. It's usually a big letdown.

The second question that people ask when you have really deceived them with a good trick is, "Would you do that again?" Don't .

I know exactly how you will feel at this point. "Wow, I really fooled them. I think I'll fool them again." Another big mistake, if you do it. You see, most tricks fool people because they don't know how it's going to end. And you should never tell them how it's going to end. Like a good joke, it's the surprise ending that really gets them.

So, if you repeat a trick they will know what to be looking for — and you'll usually get caught. Very embarrassing. And unnecessary. If you are asked to repeat a trick, say, "Well, just let me show you this one..." and go on to another miracle.

There are certain tricks which, because of their plot, are alright to repeat. You will find some of them in this book. In each case I will inform you that it is a trick you may repeat. For all the others, stick to the basic rule: *Don't repeat a trick — even if they beg you.*

Another very important thing to learn if you want to be a magician is that you must be perfect. Now that seems to be a very strong statement. After all, how many people are perfect? It is not easy to be perfect in anything you do, whether it is in your school grades or in anything you attempt.

But performing magic is different. If you do a trick and slip up in your presentation of it — if someone catches a glimpse of something that's supposed to be hidden in your hand, for instance — the whole thing is ruined.

For example, if you play piano, and hit a bad note, you just keep going — and the audience can still enjoy your performance. But you can't afford to make mistakes in conjuring.

So, what is the answer? Easy. You must practise. And practise. And practise. Until you've got it down perfectly. And how do you know when it's perfect? Try the trick in front of a mirror. And then try it for a close friend or a member of your family — someone who will give you an honest opinion. After that you've got something you can always do with complete confidence.

You may ask, "Alright, what if I do have a mishap during my performance, what then?" The answer: If it's something the audience really notices, just forget that trick, make a joke if you can, and go on to another effect. If it's a small error that no one pays much attention to, just keep going — same as the pianist.

Another one of the mistakes beginners usually make is that, when they learn the secret of a trick, it looks so easy that they can't wait to rush out and do it for someone. Just remember, no matter how simple it seems, it always requires practice. Another basic rule.

Most of the tricks in this book are of the impromptu type. Which means that they seem to be done without any preparation. I repeat: *seem* to be done. Many do require preparation ahead of time. But the audience of course isn't aware of that. This gives you a big advantage.

And one more thing. You will find that in many of the tricks I tell you what to say during the performance. What you say is sometimes very important and often has a lot to do with what you make the spectator think. And this helps make the trick work.

After you get used to the tricks, you don't have to use my exact words. Use your own expressions — as long as the meaning remains the same.

Learn just a few tricks at the beginning, but learn to do them well. Then you can call yourself a magician.

Chapter One

Card Tricks

There are probably more magic tricks using playing cards than any other type of magic you can think of.

There are several good reasons for this. Almost everyone has a deck of cards around the home. And everyone is familiar with playing cards. Also, there are few people who have not learned some kind of simple card trick as a small child.

The number of card tricks which have been invented over the years is mind-boggling. There are thousands of them. You can easily learn how to do hundreds, but you'll never remember how to do them all after you learn them.

Your best bet is to learn just a few good ones, and stick with them. Then you will become really smooth at performing these effects.

There is one type of card trick I would urge you to keep away from. That is the long drawn-out effect where you have dozens of cards dealt out, heaped in different piles, moved around, recounted — and on and on. Guaranteed to put your audience to sleep.

The best type of card trick is brief and to the point.

The tricks in this chapter are mostly easy to do, and require no special dexterity. Some of them should be practised with the cards in your hands.

So, let's go. You, too, can be a card expert.

Salted

◆ What the audience sees:

This is a super card trick that will astound your friends. Have someone shuffle a deck of cards and divide them into three or four piles. When you turn your back, have someone select any card from the middle of any pile, look at it, remember it and place it face down on top of that pile. Now, turn back and ask, "Which is your selected pile? That one? Alright, now place the other piles on top of it. Your card is now hidden. To make things more difficult for me, cut the deck two or three times."

After this, pick up the deck, hold it face down with your hand above it and release a packet of cards from the bottom of the deck into your hand and say, "Please turn over the top card of the bunch I just dropped." It will be the selected card.

◆ Preparation ahead of time:

Moiston the tip of your index finger and pour a little salt onto it. Several grains must stick to your fingertip.

◆ How the trick is presented:

When the spectator answers your question about which pile he or she has selected, point to it as you ask, "That one?" As you do that, touch the centre of the top card with your salty fingertip. A few grains of salt will remain on it.

After the deck is cut, pick it up with your thumb at one end and your middle and fourth fingers at the other end. Your hand should be arched over the deck. Hold your other hand palm up, a few inches under the deck, to catch the dropped cards. Release the pressure of your thumb ever so slightly. The deck will automatically divide where the salt is located and the bottom section will drop. Practise this, it's easy. Try it and you'll even surprise yourself.

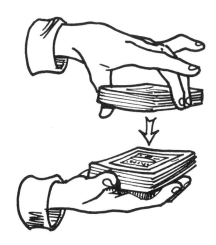

The Tens

◆ **What the audience sees:**
Remove a deck of cards from its case, hand it to a spectator saying "Please shuffle the cards." Take back the deck and replace it in its case.

Toss the case to someone else saying "Would you remove the cards and follow my instructions. Deal out four cards face down, side-by-side on the table. Now deal as many cards as you wish on top of each of those cards, using up the whole deck, so that you have four separate piles. All cards should be face down."

When this has been done, ask each of four spectators to look at, memorize and replace the top card of each pile. Now say to one of them "Assemble the four piles together and cut the deck."

At this point you pick up the deck, look through it and remove four cards. Ask each spectator to name the card he memorized. As this is done, dramatically toss down each card, one at a time. They all match.

◆ **Preparation ahead of time:**
Remove the four tens and place them top of the deck. Replace the deck in its case.

◆ **How the trick is presented:**
When you remove the cards for shuffling, let the four tens remain in the case. This must not be noticed. When you replace the shuffled deck in the case, be sure that the four tens remain at the top of the deck. The idea of carelessly tossing the case to someone gives you the reason for replacing the cards in the case. Otherwise it might look suspicious.

When the spectator deals out the first four cards, they will of course be tens, which will remain at the bottom of each pile. When the four piles are reassembled, each ten will automatically be on top of each memorized card. All you have to do is look for each ten and pull out the card under it. Remember, cutting the deck doesn't change the order of the cards. What could be easier?

Turnover

◆ What the audience sees:

Spread out a deck of cards face down on a table. Have someone select any card, look at it and remember it. Then push the cards together into a pile, still face down. Say "Place your card face down on top of the deck, then cut the deck in half and complete the cut." After this is done, tell your audience "This is very difficult. I'm going to cause one of the cards in the middle of the deck to turn over without my touching the cards."

Slap your hands together and shout "Now — turn!" Ask someone to spread out the cards again — one card will be found to be facing up. Let us suppose it's a six. Say "That is the magic card that will find the card you selected. You see, it's a six. That means you have to count down to the sixth card below the magic card. That will be you're card." When this is done, the sixth card turned over, sure enough, it will be the selected card.

◆ Preparation ahead of time:

Place one of the sixes face up near the bottom of the deck, with five cards beneath it. Of course it can be any other number you may wish. The number of cards beneath it will always be one less than the chosen number.

◆ How the trick is presented:

When you spread the cards to have one selected, be sure not to spread out the few cards at the bottom, so the face-up card is not revealed. Push forward a few cards around the middle when you say "Pick any card." This will keep people from pulling a card from the bottom, which you want to avoid. Simply follow the above instructions and the trick works automatically. Make a big thing over your calling the card to turn over. That's what makes it look like magic. Be sure to have the person who selected the card name it out loud before it is turned over at the end.

Thumbprint

What the audience sees:

Shuffle a deck of cards and hand it to someone saying, "When I turn my back, deal the cards face down on the table and stop dealing whenever you wish. Then look at and remember the top card of the pile on the table or of the pile still in your hand. Press the tip of your thumb against the face of that card before replacing it where it was."

After this is done, ask the spectator to place the cards still in his hand on top of those on the table. He must then cut the deck several times.

Then you turn back, take the cards, look through them and pass a few cards from one hand to the other. Then say, "This might be too easy...I'll do it the hard way... behind my back." Hold the deck behind you and, after a few moments, say "Ah, I've located your thumbprint."

Bring the deck forward and place it face down on the table, saying, "Now please name your card." Then you immediately show the card which was named.

Preparation ahead of time:

Really, no preparation. Just glance at the cards after you first shuffle them and remember the top and bottom cards of the deck.

How the trick is presented:

When you look through the deck after turning back to the audience, just look for the two cards you had memorized. Each time you see one, remove the card to its right and place it on top of the deck. One of those two cards will be the chosen one.

Remember the one which is now on top. When the cards are behind your back, take the top card, turn it over and place it into the middle of the deck, reversed.

Now you know that you can't miss — the chosen card has to be the one now on top of the deck or the reversed card in the middle.

After the card is named, if it's the top one, just ask someone to turn over the top card. If it's the other, just spread the deck across the table and there's the chosen card, face up in a face-down deck.

Finish by saying, "It's amazing what a powerful thumbprint you have!"

Aces

◆ What the audience sees:

Hand someone a deck of cards — it can be a borrowed deck — and say "Shuffle them, please, then drop them into my pocket." After this is done, ask someone in the audience to call out a small number, under 10. Pull out that number of cards, one at a time, from your pocket and place them face down on the table. Do not look at the faces. While doing this, say "Believe it or not, I can see right through these cards." When you come to one of the cards, stare hard at its back and say "Ah, there's one," and place it to one side, still face down. Repeat this procedure three more times. You will end up with four face-down cards set aside from the rest. Have someone turn them over. They will be the four aces.

◆ Preparation ahead of time:

Remove the four aces from the deck and place them in your jacket or pants pocket.

◆ How the trick is presented:

When the spectator places the deck in your pocket, hold the pocket open so that your hand covers the aces and they're not seen. Whatever number is selected, be sure to pull out an ace, each time you reach into your pocket. You can pretend to examine the back of every card, but stare a little longer at each ace before you set it aside. A good idea is to set aside one of the other cards at one time, then hesitate and change your mind, switching it for the ace when you pull it out.

This makes you look a little uncertain at times and makes it even more surprising when the four aces are revealed.

Pocketed

◆ What the audience sees:

Have someone shuffle a deck of cards. Take the deck and say "Now, I'm going to show you one card at a time. I'll count the cards as I show them. Just remember any one of these cards, and the number I call out for that card. Don't tell me what it is. After I've shown several cards past the one you've chosen, ask me to stop."

Then hold the cards in your left hand and take one at a time from the top in your right hand, showing the face and counting "one, two, three," etc. Suppose the spectator mentally chooses the ninth card which is the 5 of Clubs. After, say, the fifteenth card, he says "stop." Place all the cards you've shown back on top of the deck in their original position. Hold the deck behind your back, remove one card and place it in your left jacket pocket without showing the face. Bring the deck forward, saying "What was the number of the card you chose? The ninth?" Count down to the ninth card. Place it face down on a table. Have someone turn it over. It will be the wrong card. Now remove the card you had placed in your pocket. Voila, it's the 5 of Clubs.

◆ How the trick is presented:

When the deck is behind your back, take the bottom card and place it on top. Take the next bottom card and place it in your pocket. When the spectator is turning over the card on the table and everyone's attention is on it, do the following: Place the deck, which is in your left hand, halfway into your pocket. Your thumb will be over the top card, which will be the 5 of Clubs. Push downward with your left thumb and the card will drop into your pocket. Make sure it falls in front of the card already there — so when you reach in, you pull out the chosen card. This trick is easy to do — try it.

The Invisible Deck

◆ What the audience sees:

Actually, this should be entitled "what the audience doesn't see." Show a card case, open it and pretend to remove a deck of cards. It's really empty, but you say, "These cards, as you can't see, are invisible. But don't worry, they're here alright." Pretend to shuffle the cards, then say, "I'll divide the deck in half — now watch." Pretend to toss each half into the air. "See, they vanish." Now, turn slightly to your left, reach behind your right knee with your right hand, saying "And here is half the deck." Of course there is nothing there. Now turn slightly to your right, reach behind your left knee with your left hand, bring it out and presto! there is half a deck of REAL cards in your hand. Once again, reach behind your right knee, as before, and bring out the rest of the cards, saying "I told you they were here — only now you can see them."

◆ Preparation ahead of time:

You have to wear a belt and a jacket that covers it. Divide a deck of cards in half. Place one half under your belt behind you, toward your left side. Place the other half in the same position toward your right side.

◆ How the trick is presented:

When you first turn left, to reach behind your right knee, your left arm will be out of view. Simply bring that hand under your jacket and pull the cards on your left side out from under the belt. With the back of your hand towards the audience, hold them behind your left knee, then turn your hand as you bring it out to show the cards. Repeat the same actions with your right hand. Practise this. It's easy, it's entertaining and it's quite a surprise when you produce the "invisible cards."

Fingertips

 What the audience sees:
Have someone shuffle a deck of cards. Spread them face down all over the table. Have a spectator point to any card. Tell her, "I have see-through fingertips. I will tell you the name of this card without looking at the face. Please write it down."

Touch the back of the card the spectator has chosen and name it. Repeat this with two more cards. Then say, "Now I'll choose one." Touch one more card and name it . Pick up each card after you name it and set it aside, without showing the face. Finally, pick up the four cards and show them, one at a time.

Believe it or not, they all match the list the spectator marked down. Can you figure this one out before reading the explanation?

How the trick is presented:
After the deck is shuffled, take a peek at the bottom card and remember it. When you spread the cards out, keep your eye on that card and remember where it is. When the spectator points at a card, touch it, and name the bottom card which you memorized. Have the spectator write it down.

Next, pick up the card you just touched. As you set it aside, face down, peek at it. This is the card you will name when the spectator points at the next card. Then repeat again.

After three cards have been set aside in this way you will choose the last card. This will be the original bottom card of the deck. Simply name the last card you peeked at.

Now, when you finally show the four cards chosen, they will all match the list which the spectator marked down.

This may all sound a little complicated, but if you do it step by step — it works.

Phonavision

◆ What the audience sees:

This is magic over the telephone. Call a friend and ask him or her to bring a deck of cards to the phone. Have your own deck in hand. Now say "Shuffle your cards while I shuffle mine," and shuffle your deck. Then say "Would you please riffle your cards near the phone and make sure the faces are towards the phone." After this is done , say "Oh, oh — one of my cards is in the wrong place, it won't match yours. Wait a second — I'll put it in the right place in the deck."

Your friend will probably ask what you mean by that so you can explain that you have placed one of your cards in exactly the same position from the top of the deck as a matching card in his deck. Of course your friend won't believe that but just say "When you riffled your cards I got a quick look at them by phonavision, and I just matched one of my cards with one of yours. And I can prove it. Start dealing your cards one at a time from the top, face up on the table. I'll do the same with mine. We'll do one at a time together. I'll call out the name of each card as I deal. Watch your cards. At one point, our two cards will match. Let me know when this happens."

Then you both proceed as outlined in your instructions. It is amazing but what you predicted will actually happen.

◆ How the trick is presented:

When you say that you're going to move the position of one of your cards, you don't actually do anything. The whole thing works automatically. If it doesn't work the first time, just ask your friend to do it once more. It will almost certainly work the second time. It all depends on what we call the laws of probability — when you deal out two decks together, you almost always get a point at which two cards will match. Try it for yourself. Doing it over the phone makes it an even stronger trick than it otherwise would be.

Voice Recognition

◆ What the audience sees:

Have someone shuffle a deck of cards and hand it to you. Square up the pack and place it on the table. Ask the spectator to place four cards face down in a row. Then say "Deal one card at a time face down on each of these cards in rotation until you end up with the whole deck in four piles." When this is done, say "Now put piles 1 and 2 together, select any card from that pile, remember it, and place it on top of pile 3 or pile 4. Now, place all the remaining cards on top of that pile. Do all this while my back is turned."

After this is done, say "Hold the cards face up, deal them down one at a time and call out each card as you deal it. When you come to your selected card, I will tell you by the tone of your voice which is your card, no matter how hard you try to fool me."

Of course you will succeed in identifying the chosen card through your magic voice recognition system.

◆ How the trick is presented:

When you square up the cards at the beginning, glance at and remember the two bottom cards. They will end up on top of piles 3 and 4 after the deck is dealt out. So the selected card will always end up on top of one of your remembered cards. When the spectator calls out each card at the end of the routine, all you have to do is listen for one of your cards to be named. The next one will be the selected card.

Don't just say "That is your card." Make a big thing about recognizing the change in tone of the spectator's voice. The audience will really wonder if that is the way you accomplished the trick. It will really puzzle them.

Assisted by Gordon

◆ What the audience sees:

Have a card selected from a deck without anyone seeing it except the spectator who selects it. Have it placed face down on top of the deck; have the deck cut and the cut completed. Then say "Oh, I forgot, Henry Gordon taught me this trick and he said I must remove the joker from the deck."

Look through the deck and remove the joker. Then say "Mr. Gordon told me to spell out the following sentence and I will find your chosen card." Then remove a card from the top of the deck for each letter as you spell out T-H-E   C-H-O-S-E-N C-A-R-D   I-S   H-E-R-E. The last card is turned face up as you say, "And there's your card."

But it turns out to be the wrong card. Look surprised, then say, "That's all right, I was told that if this happened, I should spell out G-O-R-D-O-N   P-L-E-A-S-E H-E-L-P   M-E." Remove one card at a time from the top of the deck to spell out this latter sentence. Turn over the last card and, presto, it is the selected card. Say, "I knew Mr. Gordon wouldn't let me down!"

◆ Preparation ahead of time:

Place the joker second card from the bottom of the deck.

◆ How the trick is presented:

You can start off by shuffling the deck, but don't disturb the bottom few cards, so that the joker remains second from the bottom. When you remove the joker, take all the cards below it (after the cut is completed) and place them on top of the deck. This will place the selected card second from the top. When you do the first spelling, be sure to place the cards down one on top of the other, then place the packet on top of the deck. The second spelling will automatically bring you to the selected card. An easy to do but effective and entertaining trick.

A Spelling Lesson

◆ What the audience sees:
Spread out a deck of cards face up on a table, to show they are all different and well mixed. Close up the deck, pick it up, then fan out the cards again face up. Ask someone to select any card they see without saying anything, and to remember it. Ask "Are you good at spelling? Do you think you can spell the name of the card you selected?" Hand the deck, face down, to this person and say, "Alright, would you spell out your card, out loud, dealing one card for each letter. When you reach the last letter, turn that card over." When this is done, the last card will be the chosen one.

◆ Preparation ahead of time:
On top of a deck that is face down, place the following six cards: first, the 3 of Diamonds, then the 9 of Diamonds, the 8 of Hearts, the King of Spades, the 6 of Hearts, the 10 of Clubs. The 10 will be on top. Remove any nine other cards from the deck and place them on top of these. We're ready to go.

◆ How the trick is presented:
When you fan out the cards for a mental selection, do it in such a way that only the six specially selected cards can be clearly seen. The rest of the deck should be spread so little that none of the other card indexes are completely shown. A little practice will make this clear. Just fan the cards slowly and carefully. No matter which card is mentally selected, the trick will work.

Each prepared card spells with 10,11,12,13,14 and 15 letters respectively, so with nine cards on top, the whole thing works automatically.

Remember, the word "of" must be used in the spelling.

Example: T-E-N O-F C-L-U-B-S. You can use other prepared cards if you do it again for the same audience, as long as they spell out with the same number of letters.

Spelling the Colors

◆ What the audience sees:

Remove six red and six black cards from a deck. Place the blacks on top of the reds. Hold the packet face down. Show the faces of the black cards again, dropping them face down on the table. then drop the reds on top of them, after showing the faces — all face down. Pick up the packet, holding it face down. Spell R-E-D, moving one card at a time for each letter, from the top to the bottom of the packet. Drop the next card, face up on the table.

It will be red. Repeat the same process, spelling B-L-A-C-K. The card after the last one you drop will be black. Continue spelling RED and BLACK in turn. Every card in the packet will be correctly predicted.

◆ How the trick is presented:

After you first place the blacks on the reds, casually thumb off the top five cards and show them, saying "Here are the black ones" and drop them face down. The audience will think they've seen all the blacks. Without hesitating , push off three more cards and drop them face down on the others. Show the last four cards to be red, saying "Oh, and here are the red ones," and drop them face down on the pile on the table. If you do all of this somewhat carelessly, no one will suspect any hanky-panky. Now, pick up the entire packet and begin the spelling and the movement of cards from top to bottom. The entire effect works automatically. Look surprised and say "I didn't know cards can understand spelling!"

The Spelling Deck

Here's another great card-spelling trick.

◆ What the audience sees:

Have someone shuffle a deck of cards. Take the cards, spread them face down and have someone select one, remember it and replace it in the deck.

Have the cards cut several times. Now, pick them up and slowly spread them from hand to hand, face up, asking "Have you seen your card yet? Is it still in the deck?"

When the answer is yes, put the deck together. Now say "I'm going to name any card. Let's say the 5 of Hearts. I've taught this deck how to spell. Watch."

Deal one card at a time onto a table, from the top of the deck, spelling out the 5 of Hearts. Turn up the last card — it will be the 5 of Hearts.

Give the rest of the deck to your spectator saying, "Do the same thing. Spell out the card you selected and that card will be the last one."

When she deals the cards, spelling her secret card, she will find the last card is not the chosen one. Give the pile back to her, saying "Do it again, but speak up a little louder." When she repeats the dealing and the spelling, sure enough, the last card will be the one she selected. Quite a surprise.

◆ How the trick is presented:

After the cards are shuffled, look at and remember the bottom card, the 5 of Hearts (or any other, which you will name apparently at random when you do the trick). Have the card chosen by the spectator placed on top, undercut the bottom half of the deck and place it on top. The 5 of Hearts is now on top of the chosen card.

When you spread the cards face up, look for the 5 of Hearts. When you see it, start spelling it out to yourself as you spread the cards, one by one. When you've spelled it to the last card, just take the remaining bunch of cards and place them on the other side of the cards in your other hand (they go from the top to the bottom of the deck).

The deck is now set up so that the trick works easily. It looks a little complicated when you read about it but practise it with the cards in your hands.

It's really very easy — and very mysterious.

Magnetizing

◆ What the audience sees:

Deal out a deck of cards into six or seven piles, face down. Ask a spectator to reassemble the deck by placing the piles together in any order. Take the deck and spread the cards face down from your left to your right hand, asking the spectator to select any card, look at it, and remember it. Then replace it in the deck.

Lay the deck on a table, face down, and ask to have it cut a few times. Spread the cards on the table and say, "The card you selected will magnetically attract this pencil" as you hold a pencil over the cards.

Let one end of the pencil descend slowly while you are holding the other end, until it touches one of the cards.

Have someone turn over the card the pencil is touching. It will be the chosen card. "And remember," you say, "I have not looked at the faces of the cards at any time."

◆ Preparation ahead of time:

You must use a deck that has a picture of some kind on the back of the cards. There are many decks with pictures of animals. Those are good to use. Set up the deck so that the picture on every second card is turned upside down.

◆ How the trick is presented:

When dealing the piles, each must have an even number of cards. When a card is selected, lift the card that was below it so it becomes the bottom card in the right hand. Have the selected card replaced on top of those in the left hand. Then replace the right-hand bunch of cards on top of those in the left hand.

After you've spread the cards on the table, look for two pictures together facing in the same direction. Below them will be two others facing in the opposite direction. The first of these is the card the spectator chose.

The magnetic attraction idea makes the ending more dramatic and interesting.

Predicto

◆ What the audience sees:

Place a deck of cards face down on a table and ask someone to cut the deck in half. Look at the bottom half and say, "Now, let me see — the sixth card from the top will be the Ace of Hearts." Then count off five cards from that pile and set the sixth card aside, face down. Don't show it yet. Then look at the other pile of cards, wave your hand over it and say "The sixth card in this pile is the 5 of Clubs." Again count off five cards and place the sixth, face down, on top of the other card you had set aside. When these cards are turned, sure enough, they match your predictions.

◆ Preparation ahead of time:

Secretly look at the sixth card from the top of the deck and remember it. Let's suppose it's the Ace of Hearts.

◆ How the trick is presented:

When you look at the pile from the bottom half of the deck, everyone knows there is no way you could know the name of the sixth card. But what you are naming is the Ace of Hearts, which is actually the sixth card in the other pile, the one you set aside first. When you remove the card, secretly glance at it — let's say it's the 5 of Clubs.

Now, when you predict the second card, you name the 5 of Clubs but it's really the Ace you have removed. You have now got the two correct cards. All you have to do when you pick up the two cards is mix them as you are talking so the spectators don't know which is which. Have the cards named again, then show their faces. Right on.

Tapped

◆ What the audience sees:
Have someone shuffle a deck of cards, then remove one card, look at it, remember it and place it face down on the table. Ask her to drop the rest of the cards face down on top of the selected card. Then pick up the entire deck, shuffle it and say: "I would like you to think of a number, any number, say between 5 and 25, and tell us what it is."

After this is done (suppose the number chosen is 12), say "Alright, the deck is now face down on the table. Please tap the top card 12 times. Believe it or not, your chosen card will move to the twelfth spot from the top.

"But before you do this, you can change your mind and select another number if you wish."

After the tapping has been done, and whether another number has been selected or not, say: "I will now count down to the magic number."

Count down 12 cards (if the number 12 was finally selected; if not, whatever number was selected) onto your right hand and drop them all on top of the deck. The top card will now be the last one counted — the twelfth card. Turn it over with a flourish. Oh-oh, you are wrong: It is not the selected card.

"Oh I think I know what went wrong," you explain. "You tapped the deck with the wrong finger. Try your little finger. That should do it."

The spectator again taps the top card 12 times. Say "Perhaps you would like to count down to the twelfth card yourself." The spectator now does so and guess what? It is the selected card!

◆ How the trick is presented:
When you pick up the cards to shuffle them, after the card was selected and dropped on the table, that card will of course be at the bottom of the deck. Do an overhand shuffle and end by dropping the last card (the bottom card) on top.

The selected card will now be on top of the deck. When you first count off 12 cards, you will be reversing the order of the cards as you do so. So you will automatically be placing the selected card in the twelfth position. You are now set for the second countdown, which will find the right card.

Some of the best tricks are so simple, aren't they? When you know the secret!

Dice Directory

◆ What the audience sees:

Hand two dice to a spectator, saying "Take these dice, toss them on the table after I turn my back to you. Remember the number on top of one of them, then cover it with a cup. Leave the other uncovered."

Let us suppose the hidden number is 3. Then direct the spectator to pick up a deck of cards and shuffle them — all this with your back turned. Say "Whatever the hidden number is, count down that number of cards from the top of the deck and remember the card at that number." He will then note the number of the third card.

Have him give you the deck while your hands are behind your back. Turn around and say, "Now, by looking at the number of the visible die, I will get a message. I will remove your card, behind my back, and place it in another location in the deck."

Suppose the visible die shows a 5. Now have the number on the hidden die revealed. The numbers 3 and 5 add up to 8. Ask someone to count down eight cards from the top of the deck and then turn over the next card.

Believe it or not, it will be the previously chosen card.

◆ How the trick is presented:

When you turn back to face the audience, keep the cards in your hands behind your back. As you look at the number on the visible die, which is 5, transfer five cards from the bottom of the deck to the top, then transfer one more card. Bring the deck forward and place it on the table. Remind your audience, "Remember, I had no idea where your chosen card was in the deck." They will be quite surprised when the card is found in the new location. This is one trick that can be repeated if you wish. It's pretty hard to figure out.

Do It with Mirrors

◆ What the audience sees:

Place a book on a table in front of you. Take a deck of cards and remove the four aces. Show them, then replace them in the deck in different places. Shuffle the cards. Now say "I'm going to show you how gamblers cheat at cards. I will place this tiny mirror behind the book so you can't see it."

Put an unseen item in your hand on your side of the book (the audience should be seated at the other side of the table). Begin dealing out the cards face down, saying "As I deal, I can see the faces of the cards reflected in the mirror."

As you deal through the deck, you will put four cards aside at intervals, face down. Say "And this is how gamblers know where the aces are," as you turn over the four cards. They will be the four aces.

The real surprise comes when you say, "As a magician, I can do something the gamblers can't do — make the mirror disappear." Remove the book and, presto, the mirror is gone.

◆ Preparation ahead of time:

This is another super trick with a deck of cards that has pictures on the backs of the cards. Be sure they're all facing in the same direction before you start.

◆ How the trick is presented:

When you replace the four aces in the deck after showing them, all you have to do is reverse each card so the picture on the back faces the opposite way from the rest of the cards. When you deal out the cards, just look for the reversed pictures. These are the aces. Just set them aside. Of course, there never is a mirror. But be sure to make a good pretense of placing one behind the book. To be more realistic, after you "place it down," pretend to look into it and smooth down your hair.

This is a very entertaining trick.

Lie Detector

◆ **What the audience sees:**
A spectator chooses a card from a deck, remembers it and replaces it in the deck. You ask the spectator to tell you if you are right or wrong as you name all the suits or numbers in turn. He can lie or tell the truth each time. At the end you tell him that you knew when he lied, and you name the card he chose.

◆ **Preparation ahead of time:**
Separate all the black and all the red cards. Put the deck together with all the reds on top.

◆ **How the trick is presented:**
Fan out the deck, faces down, but only fan out the top half. That way a red card must be chosen.

While the unsuspecting spectator is looking at his card, square up the pack, then fan out the bottom half, where he will place his card. Pretty sneaky, eh?

Now look through the faces, saying, "Let's see if I can find your card." You seem to fail, of course, but at the same time you spot the card — the red card stands out like a beacon among all the blacks. Shuffle up the deck as you say: "I'm going to call out the suits and then the numbers.

"You must answer yes or no for each one. You can be truthful or lie. I can always tell."

At the end, you name the chosen card which you knew all along. But the "lie detector" bit makes it really interesting.

Do Your Own Thing

◆ What the audience sees:

Have a spectator shuffle a deck of cards and give you about half the deck, keeping the rest for herself. Turn your back and say, "Take any card from your packet, look at it, remember it and place it face down on top of the packet."

When she has done this, turn around and place your packet on top of hers. She is now holding the whole deck. Ask her to hold the cards behind her back. Make sure she is standing so that no one can see the deck.

Then say, "Take off the top card and place it at the bottom of the deck. Now take the current top card, reverse it and push it into the middle of the deck."

Next, have her bring the deck forward and place it face down on the table. Spread all the cards out across the table so that they barely overlap one another.

One card will be seen reversed (wrongside up) around the middle of the deck. Say "Please name the card you chose." After it is named, have her turn over the first card beneath the reversed card. It will be the chosen card.

◆ How the trick is presented:

While the spectator is choosing her card, and your back is turned, you are holding your packet in front of you, away from her and from the audience. Secretly reverse the card on the bottom of your packet and also reverse the card second from the top. Just look downward with your eyes, don't bend your head, so you won't seem to be doing anything with the cards.

After that, the spectator is really doing the trick for you. When she reverses a card, she is putting back the card you had reversed into its normal face-down position, so that it's lost in the deck. The card that is finally seen reversed is the one you reversed at the bottom of your packet, but everyone will think it's the one the spectator reversed.

This is a good trick because the spectator seems to be finding her own card magically.

Matchup

◆ What the audience sees:

Hand a deck of cards to a spectator and ask her to cut the deck approximately in half, to keep the bottom half and give the top half back to you. Place both packs face down on the table. Then, turn your back and say, "Take any number of cards up to ten from your pack and place them on top of my pack." Turn back to face your partner, pick up your pack and fan the cards, still face down. Pull out one card and show its face. The number on that card will be the same as the number of cards that were transferred. It always works!

◆ Preparation ahead of time:

Remove ten cards from a deck — an Ace, a 2, a 3, all the way up to number 10. They can be of any suit, Clubs, Hearts, etc. Place them in order on top of the deck, starting with the Ace. The 10 will now be on top of the deck. Place any other three cards on top of the 10. Remember, they're all face down. You're all set to go.

◆ How the trick is presented:

After the spectator has transferred the cards and you pick up your pack, spread out your cards. Now, as you fan the cards, mentally count them from the top until you spot the fourteenth card. That's the card you pull out and show. Its number will always match the number of transferred cards. As soon as you're done, shuffle the deck. This mixes up the cards you originally lined up. You have now destroyed the evidence should anyone wish to examine the deck.

Clipped

What the audience sees:

Remove the four queens from a deck of cards. Show them, then place them in the middle of the deck. Toss the entire pack into a paper bag and twist the top of the bag so that it is closed. Hand the bag to a spectator, saying "Shake up the bag well. We want the cards to be really mixed up." Take back the bag, holding it high so that you can't look inside. Open it and reach inside with one hand. Rummage around and say "Ah, this feels like a queen." Pull out a card and show it. It is a queen. Repeat this three more times. Unbelievable. You have found the four queens in the mixed-up mess of cards.

Preparation ahead of time:

Have a paper bag ready. Hide a paper clip between the thumb and forefinger of your right hand.

How the trick is presented:

When you first show the four queens, place them in your right hand, sliding them into the paper clip as you do so. You can fan them out slightly to show them. Your thumb will conceal the clip. Square them up with your left hand and place them into the middle of the deck. Your audience will not realize that they are all clipped together. After the cards are dropped into the bag, it doesn't matter how much the bag is shaken up, the four queens will remain clipped together.

Now, when you reach inside, first place the clipped queens on top of the other cards to keep them separated from the others. Then pull out one queen at a time, pretending to search for each one. Let the clip remain at the bottom of the bag. The only thing to practise is hiding the clip in your hand at the beginning.

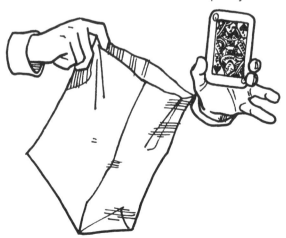

Reverso

◆ What the audience sees:

Hand a deck of cards to a spectator, turn away and say "Please shuffle the cards. Now count off any number of cards fewer than 15. Look at and remember the last card you counted and place all the cards back on the deck in the same order."

Now turn back, take the deck, hold it behind your back and say: "I'll now try to find your card." After a minute or two, bring the deck forward.

Say "No luck. Will you please take the cards and count off the same number of cards you did before, then place them at the bottom of the deck?

"You can look at the cards you're counting — your chosen card is not among them, because I've mixed up the cards."

Now take back the deck, hold it behind your back again saying "I'll try again."

After a moment or two, bring the deck forward, saying: "There's only one way to do this."

Spread the cards face down across the table top. One card will be face up in the middle of the deck. It will be the chosen card.

◆ How the trick is presented:

When you first hold the deck behind your back, count off 15 cards from the top of the deck without reversing their order. Place them on the bottom. Pretend that you failed to find the card.

The second time that the deck is behind you, count 15 cards from the bottom and place them on the top of the deck. The chosen card will now be on the bottom. Simply take the bottom card, turn it over and push it into the middle of the deck. The rest is showmanship. The sudden appearance of a face-up card in a face-down deck is always a surprise. This is another easy-to-do trick which is quite baffling.

Chapter Two
Money Magic

I wonder why everyone seems to enjoy magic tricks done with money. Could it be because money is a nice thing to have? Or perhaps we would all like to be able to conjure up money whenever we need it.

However, the idea for this book is to be able to do magic with objects easily obtained. And there is always some money around — even if it's only a few pennies. By the way, there are some excellent tricks in this chapter done with just a few pennies. Of course if you want real class, there are also tricks using dollar bills.

Coin magic is really a field in itself. In the past there have been several great and famous magicians who have specialized in doing magic with nothing but coins. Indeed, there are several of these conjurers practising today.

Most of them use complicated and difficult sleight-of-hand. If you continue with your magic hobby, you can begin to learn some of this wonderful magic as you progress.

In this chapter, however, we are going to learn money magic that's easy to perform — and will still mystify and entertain. Just keep a little loot in your pocket or purse, and you'll be ready to do magic wherever you go.

X-Ray Vision

◆ **What the audience sees:**
Show three coins (quarters are good) to the spectator. Mark one of these coins with a pencil. Show three walnut half shells. Go out of the room while a spectator covers each coin with a shell. Come back in and put on a pair of "X-ray glasses." You can immediately point to the shell which covers the marked coin. This can be repeated.

◆ **Preparation ahead of time:**
Take three quarters. Glue a small piece of hair to the bottom of one of them. About a half inch of hair should stick out past the edge of the coin. Get a few walnuts. Open them carefully and proceed to eat them. That's not part of the trick but why waste good nuts? Now, save three half-shells and clean them out. So we have the three shells and three quarters (one with the hair attached).

◆ **How the trick is presented:**
Place the quarters on a table, the gimmicked one with the hair side down. Mark that coin. When the coins are covered with the shells you can spot the marked one because the hair sticks out past the edge of the shell.

You will see it because you're looking for it. No one else will notice it. The "X-ray glasses" are regular sun glasses but a little bit of showmanship makes every trick look better.

Coin and Hank

◆ What the audience sees:

Borrow a quarter and hold it with the tips of your left hand thumb and forefinger, about level with your shoulder. With your right hand, pick up a handkerchief at the middle of one edge and let it hang down from your hand. Hold the hanky in front of the quarter, that is, between the coin and your audience. Draw the hanky back toward yourself, swooshing it over the left hand and the quarter. When it clears your left hand, the spectators will see that the coin has vanished. Pretend to be concealing it in your left hand, then, when challenged, open your hand and show that it is empty. Your right hand is then shown to be empty and the hanky can be examined.

◆ How the trick is presented:

As your right hand draws the handkerchief over your left hand, and just when your right hand approaches the quarter, clip it between your right thumb and forefinger. This will not be seen as the hanky is covering it ! Continue drawing the hanky back without stopping. As your right hand comes to your chest, drop the coin into your breast pocket or into the open neck of your blouse or shirt. Everyone should be so busy watching your empty left hand, they will not notice you ditching the coin. The trick is done and it's easy. A complete vanish. You will be amazed at how your audience is completely deceived.

Change

◆ What the audience sees:

Place a new $1 bill on the table. Place a quarter on the centre of the bill, then neatly fold the bill into a small packet around the quarter.

Pick up the packet and say, "Just for a change, I'd like to make change in a magical way." Shake the packet a few times, lay it down on the table, and slowly unfold the $1 bill.

Instead of the quarter, you will now have two dimes and a nickel. Quite a surprise.

◆ Preparation ahead of time:

Get two new dollar bills. Lie one down with the Queen's face down. Put a spot of rubber cement on the centre of its back.

Place the second bill on top of it, so the edges match, with the Queen's face up. Press the centre so that the two bills stick together.

Fold the top one into thirds, lengthwise, then fold the top and bottom edges so they meet at the centre. Press the edges good and sharp.

Turn the bills over and repeat the same folding pattern with the other bill. Make sure the outside edges of both bills match, so that it looks like one bill when they are both folded.

Now, open one bill and place the dimes and nickel in the centre, then fold the bill around the coins. Open the other bill. You're ready to go.

◆ How the trick is presented:

When you remove the bills from your pocket or purse, hold the open bill toward the audience, with the folded one toward you so that it won't be spotted. Place them on the table with the folded side down.

Place the quarter in the centre of the open bill and fold the dollar. That's easy, because the folds are already prepared.

Pick up the (double) packet, and as you are talking, turn it over as you lay it down again.

The turning over part of the trick should not be noticed. Now, of course, when you unfold this bill, you are disclosing the dimes and the nickel you placed in there before.

If you wish, you can repeat the trick the other way, turning the two dimes and nickel back into the original quarter.

Heads and Tails

 What the audience sees:
Place 12 pennies on a table side by side. Turn your back to the table and say, "Please slide the coins around so they are all well mixed." When the spectator has done that, reach behind your back and remove six pennies, one at a time, stacking them one on top of the other as you take them in your hand.

Now say, "Please cover the pennies left on the table with your hands." Turn back to the table, bring your hands forward and place your pennies down side by side, one at a time. Say, "I now have the same number of heads-up coins as you have, and also the same number of tails-up coins. Isn't that strange?"

Ask the spectator to check the coins that have been covered. You will be absolutely correct.

 How the trick is presented:
When you first place the pennies on the table, be sure that six are heads-up and six tails-up. Mix them so this isn't noticed. When you pick up the coins, be careful that you don't turn any over as you stack them in your hand.

When you turn back to face the audience, and your hands are still behind your back, out of sight, simply turn the stack of coins over. The coins that were originally heads up will now be tails up and the tails will now be heads, when you lay them down.

When you place the pennies on the table, the number of heads and tails will automatically match those covered by the spectator. You can use any even number of coins for this trick but I suggest no fewer than 12 and not more than 16.

This is one trick you can repeat. It seems simple but it's a very clever idea. All you need are a few coins and you can do it any time, anywhere.

Burned Bill

◆ What the audience sees:
Borrow a dollar bill from someone. Read off the serial number and ask someone to write it down. Fold up the bill and place it in any envelope which you then seal and place on a table. Remove a playing cardcase from your pocket and place it, too, on the table.

Then put the envelope into an ashtray, put a lighted match to it and wait until it is completely destroyed. Say "Oh, I'm sorry — was that your dollar bill in the envelope? Well, don't worry. Just look inside the cardcase."

When the case is opened, there is the dollar bill inside — and the serial number matches.

◆ Preparation ahead of time:
Have a cardcase with a dollar bill inside it, in your left pocket. Memorize the serial number on that bill. Prepare a large ashtray on a table with a small envelope.

◆ How the trick is presented:
When you read out the serial number on the borrowed bill, you actually call out the memorized numbers from the bill in your pocket. Everyone will believe you are calling out the numbers of the bill you are looking at. Then fold the bill the same way the other one is folded.

Pick up the envelope with your left hand, while your right fingers are holding the folded bill. Pretend to place the bill in the envelope but actually, you must conceal it behind the envelope, holding it against the envelope with your left thumb. After you seal the envelope, place your left hand in your pocket to remove the cardcase, dropping the bill in your pocket at the same time.

This requires a little practice but it is not difficult. The rest is showmanship.

Quarter Caper

◆ What the audience sees:

Hold your hands out, palms up. Close your fists after someone places a quarter in each palm. Don't turn your hands over. Have another quarter placed on the closed fingers of each fist. Say "I will now attempt a difficult feat — to turn over my hands and try to grab the outside coin into each fist, ending up with two coins in each hand.

You try this, but the outside coins fall to the table. You try it again. You fail again. "I should have practised," you say, "let me try it one last time."

The third time it works. Now you say, "Now with two coins in each hand, I'm going to try some real magic." With fists still closed, you pretend to toss a coin in the air from your left hand. "Now I'll catch this invisible coin in my right hand," you say, as you pretend to do so. Then slowly open your right fist and drop three coins onto the table. Open your left fist and, believe it or not, only one quarter remains.

◆ How the trick is presented:

When you first try to catch the two outside coins, you deliberately let them fall to the table. Open your fists to show there is still a quarter in each hand. Close your fists again. The second time you actually catch the right hand coin into your fist, but the left-hand fist drops two quarters, both the one on top and the one inside. Close both fists immediately.

Everyone thinks the two coins on the table are the ones that were on top of each fist. Now, on the third try, when the two coins are placed back on your fingers, you really do grab one into each hand.

This gives you one in the left hand, three in the right.

The trick is done. The rest is showmanship. This little miracle takes some practice but it's worth it.

What's a Friend For?

What the audience sees:

This trick should be presented to an audience of at least six people. First, roll up your sleeves. Have someone place a coin on the palm of your right hand. Ask someone else to drape a handkerchief over that hand. Go around to a few spectators, asking each one in turn to place a hand under the handkerchief to make sure the coin is still there.

After three or four people have checked it, say, "Would someone please take this rubber band, gather the hanky around my wrist and place the band around my wrist." You will now have the hand containing the coin tightly bound by the handkerchief. Say, "Under these impossible conditions, I will now attempt to make the coin vanish."

Wave your left hand over the bound one, counting "One, two, three." With your left hand, touch the coin through the hanky. Say "Oh, oh. It hasn't happened yet. Let me try again. I must be using the wrong numbers."

Wave and count again. "Four, five, six. Aha! I think it happened.

"Would someone please remove the rubber band and the handkerchief, very slowly."

After this is done comes the big surprise. The coin will be gone.

Preparation ahead of time:

Have the handkerchief, rubber band and coin ready.

How the trick is presented:

Among the audience you must have a friend who will be your secret helper.

He or she will be the last one to check the coin under the hanky — and will secretly remove it. Make sure to practise with your assistant beforehand. No one ever guesses the secret, particularly if you first seem to fail to make the coin vanish. They will really believe it's been in your hand all the time.

The Queen Flips

◆ **What the audience sees:**
Hold a dollar bill between your hands with the Queen's picture facing the audience — right side up, of course. Fold the bill in half, then in quarters, then in eighths. At no time do your turn it over. Then unfold it. The Queen's picture mysteriously has turned upside down.

◆ **How the trick is presented:**
This is easy to do but not to describe, so follow these instructions carefully with a dollar bill in your hands. With the Queen's picture facing the audience, first fold the bill in half lengthwise by bending the top edge forward and down. Now, bring the right side forward and to the left side. The bill is now in quarters.

Then repeat the same move, bringing the right side forward and to the left. The bill is now in eighths.

While you are doing all this, tell your audience: "Watch carefully, I'm doing this slowly and at no time am I turning the bill over."

Now comes the important part, as you slowly unfold the bill. You actually do it a little differently from the way you folded it. With your right thumb at the left edge of the folded bill, unfold the first section facing you. This will be a double thickness. Then unfold the rest of the doubled bill with your left hand.

Now we are left with the bill folded in half lengthwise, as it was after the first fold was made. The difference is that in unfolding it, we have reversed back and front. Slowly lift the bottom edge of the side facing the audience. The Queen is now upside down. Amazing. It's important to do all the folding and unfolding very slowly, so that the audience sees that you are not pulling a fast one!

A Trickless Trick

◆ What the audience sees:

Drop about 30 pennies on a table and say "Sometimes I can do strange things. Let's try this. When I turn my back, please pick up a few pennies, say between five and ten, and count them and hide them in your hand."

Let's say eight pennies have been picked up and secretly counted. After this is done, turn around, pick up at least a dozen pennies (let's say you have 15).

Next, you say: "Alright, through my powers I already know how many pennies you have. Now I have exactly the amount you have, *plus* enough to make 12 and I have three left over. Please count your pennies onto the table."

The spectator counts eight pennies. Then you say "Exactly right. See, I have eight pennies here, the same as you, plus enough to make 9, 10, 11, 12 and I have 1, 2, 3 left over. Just what I predicted. I told you I can do strange things."

◆ How the trick is presented:

This is a strange trick because it actually requires no trickery — that's right, a trick without a trick. Everything depends on the words you say. It works by itself. When you direct the spectator to pick up the pennies and you say "let's say between five and ten," say it in an off-hand manner as if it doesn't matter to you how many she picks up. But she will follow your directions.

Now you must be sure to pick up more pennies than the spectator did, in other words, several more than 10. Your key words are, "I have exactly the amount you have plus enough to make _ and I have _ left over."

Subtract a small number from the total you picked up and that will give you the required numbers to fill in the blanks.

Of course you don't really know how many pennies the spectator actually has but it doesn't matter — the effect is that you do. This is the type of trick you should never repeat — they might catch on if you do.

Coin Vanish

◆ What the audience sees:

Hold a glass half-filled with water so that it stands on the palm of your left hand. Have someone hold a coin through the centre of a handkerchief, then drape the hanky over the glass and your hand, still holding the coin above the glass. Now say "When I count to three, release your grip on the coin and let it drop into the glass. One-Two-Three." When the coin is released, everyone will hear it click as it falls into the glass, which is concealed by the hanky. Have the hanky removed and the coin can be seen lying in the glass of water. Cover the glass again, lift it through the hanky with your right hand and place it on a table, still covered by the hanky. Now, with your left hand, whip away the hanky and — guess what — the coin has vanished.

◆ How the trick is presented:

When the spectator releases the coin, tilt the glass beneath the hanky slightly towards yourself. Instead of falling into the glass, the coin will hit the side of the glass and drop into your palm. The tinkling sound will make everyone think it actually fell into the glass. Before removing the hanky, grasp the glass through the hanky with your right hand and move it slightly so that it covers the coin. When the hanky is removed, the coin can be seen through the water and the bottom of the glass and the illusion is that it is resting inside the glass. When you replace the glass on the table, the coin remains concealed in your left palm. Use that hand to pull away the handkerchief and then drop the coin with the handkerchief into your pocket. All that's left is a glass of water. The coin has mysteriously disappeared.

Boxed

◆ What the audience sees:

Show a small matchbox. Slide open the drawer of the matchbox to reveal that it's filled with pennies. Say "Amazing what you find in matchboxes these days."

Pull the drawer all the way out and turn it over, dumping all the pennies on a table. Close the box and leave it on the table. Then pick up a penny from the pile on the table with your right hand, place it in your left hand and close your left hand over it.

Now, wave your left fist over the matchbox saying "Go, go, go."

Open your left hand and show that the penny has vanished. Slowly push open the drawer of the matchbox and, voila, there is the missing penny. It's magic!

◆ Preparation ahead of time:

You can buy small matchboxes at your favorite variety store. Remove the matches from one and glue a penny onto the inside bottom of the drawer. Then fill the drawer with pennies, covering your glued penny.

◆ How the trick is presented:

When you empty the drawer of pennies, turn it upside down and shake it to show it's really empty. The glued penny will remain in place, of course. Be careful not to show it when you empty the drawer and tilt it towards you when you slide the drawer back into the box so it won't be seen. Also, be sure to place the box on the table right side up.

When you place your right hand fingertips into the pile of pennies in order to pick one up, partially lift one but then let it slide back among the pennies as you raise your hand. It will seem that your thumb is holding it behind your fingers but there's really nothing there.

As you pretend to place the nonexistent penny in your left hand, quickly close your left fist and act as if you are now holding the coin there. Be sure to show both hands empty before opening the matchbox.

After you show the penny inside, drop the rest of the coins on top of it, close the box and drop it in your pocket.

Switcheroo

◆ What the audience sees:

Borrow a dollar bill from a member of your audience. First, have the person fold the bill in half, then fold it again, then once more. This will leave a folded strip about one half inch wide. Have her fold the strip in half, lengthwise, then take the bill.

Hold it behind your back and say, "I have very sensitive fingertips. I will now unfold the bill and by touching the serial number, I will tell you what it is. I had you fold it so that I couldn't see the number. Take a paper and pencil and write out the numbers as I call them out."

Proceed to do so. The bill is still behind your back. Then toss out the bill and have the amazed audience check your figures. Magically, they will match.

◆ Preparation ahead of time:

Take a dollar bill and memorize the serial number. Fold it as described above and slip it under the band of your wristwatch, or under a rubber band placed around your wrist. You must, of course, wear a jacket or sweater to cover your wrist.

◆ How the trick is presented:

After the bill is borrowed and folded, place it behind your back. Remove your own bill from its hiding place and place the borrowed dollar under the wristband. While doing this, begin talking about your sensitive fingertips and calling out the numbers which you memorized. Then return the dollar bill to the lender who will think it's the one he gave you.

It's the old switcheroo — and it works.

Chapter Three

Mathematical Magic

When you think of mathematics I'm sure you think of school, of studying, of working out difficult problems, and so on.

I wonder how many people realize how much fun you can have with mathematics. First of all, there are hundreds, even thousands, of puzzles using mathematics. There are loads of books and newspaper articles on the subject. There are many, many games using maths.

And speaking of mathematical puzzles, it seems that there are many magicians, including myself, who take a great interest in them. Perhaps it's because people who are interested in magic are people who like to keep their brains busy, and who are curious about things.

To be curious is a wonderful thing. It makes you want to learn things — no matter what the subject. The fact that you are now holding this book shows that you are curious — a good sign.

Apart from puzzles and games, mathematics lends itself very well to magic tricks. That's what this chapter is about.

Some of the tricks use cards or coins, but they are mathematically oriented. That's why they are included in this chapter. When you do these tricks always stress the mathematical angle.

Remember, make up your own patter as you present these math miracles.

Magic Numbers

◆ What the audience sees:

Give small slips of paper to several spectators. Ask them to jot down a three-digit number on each slip. Then tell them to fold each slip in half, drop it into a container such as a hat or a bowl. Have someone mix the slips, then you reach in, take out a slip and hand it to a spectator. Give the same person a sheet of paper and say, "Please write down the numbers from the slip onto this large paper."

Next, have someone else reach into the container, remove another slip and hand it to the same person. Say "Now write the three numbers from this slip under the other three, then multiply the two together."

While the spectator is beginning to do this, take a piece of paper, jot down a few numbers and in a moment, announce the product of the multiplication of the two numbers — which you have arrived at "by magic."

The spectator, meanwhile, will still be busy doing his multiplication — long after you have announced the right answer!

◆ Preparation ahead of time:

Take a slip of paper which matches the others and write down the number 143. Fold the paper in half, the same way you direct the others to be folded. Now, conceal this paper in your right hand.

◆ How the trick is presented:

When you reach into the container for the first slip, secretly drop the concealed slip among the others, then pick it up and take it out, with your right hand of course. It will appear that you removed one of the slips that already was there. When the second slip is given to the spectator during the calculations, have him announce the numbers on it. Suppose they are 354. Write down the number twice 354,354. Divide by 7. This will take only a few seconds. You will immediately have the magic answer.

Getting the Edge

◆ **What the audience sees:**
On a thin card, write the numerals from 1 to 9, three across, in three rows. Now, carefully tear the card into nine pieces, with a number in each. Someone must drop all the pieces into a hat and mix them. Place your hand into the hat, saying: "What would you like me to produce, the odd or even numbers?" Someone says "odd." You pull out several pieces and show them to be the 1, 3, 5, 7, 9. "Magic numbers," you tell your audience.

◆ **How the trick is presented:**
If you examine the pieces of a numbered card torn in the way I describe, you will see that all the even numbers have three rough edges, where they have been torn. The odd numbers have two rough edges, except the 5, which, being in the centre, has four rough edges.

So when you reach into the container to get the odd numbers, you just have to feel for pieces with two or four rough edges. To speed things up, when you feel pieces with three rough edges, don't drop them back, keep them in your hand until you've picked up all the odd numbers. Then drop all the evens before you bring out your hand with the odds. Of course, if even numbers are called for, just feel for the pieces with three rough edges.

Quick Calculation

◆ What the audience sees:

Ask a spectator, whose age you cannot know, to remove some loose change from her pocket and to count off any amount under a dollar and keep it in her hand. She's not to tell you the amount.

Now say, "I'm going to ask you to do some simple mathematics. Please take this paper and pencil. Now multiply your age by 2. Add 5 to the result, then multiply the total by 50. Have you got it? Now, subtract the number of days in a year from your total. That's 365, remember?

"Now," you continue, "add the total amount of change in your hand to the last result. You can now announce the final figure you have written down. Thank you."

When this is done, write something on a piece of paper and hand it to the spectator, saying: "I have just written down your age and the amount of change you are holding. Am I correct?"

And you will be!

"Isn't it amazing," you say, "I just make these magic guesses and they always seem to be accurate."

◆ Preparation ahead of time:

Have paper and pencils ready for you and the spectator.

◆ How the trick is presented:

Let us suppose the spectator is 12 years old and is holding 55 cents. After all the mathematics is completed, the number called out will be 1140.

All you have to do is secretly add 115 to the number, whatever it is. In the case of the 12-year-old, you will get a total of 1255. The first two digits will give you the person's age — the last two digits will give you the amount of the change.

On a separate piece of paper, write: "Your age is 12. You are holding 55 cents."

This is so easy to do but it's really surprising. And this is one trick you can repeat if you wish!

Tap-A-Number

◆ What the audience sees:

On a sheet of paper, draw three vertical lines from top to bottom, dividing the paper in four equal sections. Then repeat this with three horizontal lines, equally spaced. You will now have the paper divided into 16 squares.

Write the following numbers in each square. Top row, left to right: 1, 15, 3, 11. Next row, 5, 11, 7, 1. Next row, 9, 3, 5, 13. Bottom row, 13, 7, 15, 9.

Ask a spectator to think of one of the numbers on the paper, but not to name it. Now say "I'm going to tap my pencil randomly on different numbers. Count to yourself on each tap, but begin with one number higher than the one you are thinking of.

"For example," you say, "if the number you are thinking of is 10, you will think of 11 on my first tap, 12 on my second and so on.

"When you reach 25, just say STOP."

When all this is done and the spectator says STOP, your pencil will be resting on the number he was thinking of, in this case 10.

This startling trick can be repeated.

◆ How the trick is presented:

For the first nine taps, you can randomly touch any number you wish. But the tenth tap must be on the number 15.

Then you must follow this order: the 11th tap on any number, the 12th on number 13, the 13th on any number, the 14th on number 11, the 15th on any number, the 16th on number 9, the 17th on any number, the 18th on number 7, the 19th on any number, the 20th on number 5, the 21st on any number, the 22nd on number 3, the 23rd on any number, the 24th on number 1.

This list is easy to remember. You will notice the numbers you must remember begin at 13, and they are all odd numbers and that they get progressively smaller.

Your pencil will automatically fall on the selected number when the spectator reaches the mental count of 25. Be sure to tap each number slowly and carefully so that it's quite clear that you are on the chosen number when you stop.

No matter how many times you repeat this trick, they'll never be able to figure it out.

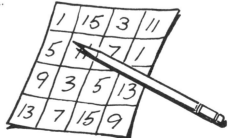

Mathemagic

What the audience sees:

Ask someone to think of a number between one and 10. Hand her a deck of cards and ask her to shuffle them. Then tell her, "Count down as many cards as the number you thought of, from the top, see the card at the number, leave it at the same position but remember it."

Keep your back turned so that you cannot observe any of this. Turn around after this is done, take the cards, hold them behind your back, saying, "This may seem impossible but I'm going to locate your card and replace it at number 20 in the deck, without even looking at the cards."

Then bring the cards forward and ask your assistant, "What was the number you thought of?" Suppose it was the number 5. Start counting from the top of the deck, beginning with 5. When you reach the number 20, place that card aside, face down. Ask for the chosen card to be named. Have the card turned over — it will be the same.

How the trick is presented:

After you place the cards behind your back, secretly count off 19 cards, reversing their order as you do so. Replace them on top of the deck. The card which had been on top is now 19th from the top. Bring the cards forward and continue as described. The audience will be baffled when the card is turned over and revealed to be the chosen one.

We call this a mathematical card trick. Even though it works automatically, don't just do it without thinking. Figure out what makes it work. It's more fun that way.

Math Miracle

What the audience sees:

Hand your pocket calculator to a spectator and ask her to enter a three-digit number on it, to press the multiply button and then the number 7. Then say, "Press the 'equals' button and give the calculator to someone else."

Now you ask the second person to press the multiply button, then the buttons to make the number 11, then the equals button.

Pass the calculator to a third person, ask him to push the multiply button, then the buttons to make the number 13, and finally the equals button.

Now you take back the calculator and say: "I will now tell you the original three-digit number which was entered." And you will!

How the trick is presented:

Many people have calculators these days. You should easily be able to borrow one for this trick. Be sure to turn your back when the first three-digit number is entered so that no one can say you peeked. After all the button-pushing has been done, take back the calculator and look at the first three digits of the final total. That will be the number you call out.

It works automatically. As soon as you memorize the numbers, erase the total. Now nobody can check the total and perhaps notice the first three numbers. This is a real puzzler for your audience and is super-easy to do!

Memory Calculation

What the audience sees:

Give someone a sealed envelope to hold. Show that a pocket calculator works normally by adding a few numbers and showing the total. Erase the total, then cover the screen with a piece of masking tape. Say "I'd like four volunteers to each think of a two-digit number." Then hand the calculator to each volunteer in turn, asking each to punch in the number and then press the PLUS button. Have the last person press the EQUALS button after his number is entered. Then remove the tape and ask a spectator to read out the total on the screen. Tell the person with the envelope "Open the envelope and read out the prediction I entered earlier." She will pull out a piece of paper and, to everyone's amazement, find the same number written on it as is show on the calculator.

Preparation ahead of time:

You must have a calculator with a Memory feature. Before your performance, punch in a three-digit number between 100 and 350. Press the "M+" button, which will store the number. Then press the ERASE button, which will clear the screen. Write the same number on a paper and seal it in an envelope.

How the trick is presented:

After the last person has pressed the EQUALS button, take back the calculator with your left hand. As you remove the tape with your right hand, press the "RM" (Recall Memory) button with your left thumb. This will flash your predicted number on the screen. Of course, everyone thinks that is the total of the numbers they punched in!

Math Wizardry

What the audience sees:
Hand someone a calculator and say, "If you look at the numbers, you'll see that they are arranged in three columns down and three rows across. What I'd like you to do is select any column or any row, or even any three numbers that form a diagonal line.

"Now, please punch in the three numbers you selected, in any order you like. Don't let me see your selection.

"You've done that? Now press the multiply sign, select another line of numbers and enter them. Then press the equals sign." You are now looking at the product of your calculation.

"There is no way I, or anyone else, can know what that number is. Will you now please mentally select one digit from that answer, but not a zero, and write it down. All done? Good.

"Please call out the remaining digits, in any order you like."

When this is done, write down the numbers that are called out. Take a quick look at them and say: "Through my rapid magic mathematics, I will now name the number you have written down."

And to everyone's amazement, you immediately do so.

Preparation ahead of time:
Have a calculator and a couple of pencils and some paper on hand.

How the trick is presented:
Suppose that the spectator selected the middle row of 4-5-6 and entered it as 4-6-5. Suppose he then chose the diagonal line of 1-5-9 and entered it as 9-1-5. The multiplication would give you the answer 4-2-5-4-7-5. Suppose the spectator chose to write down the digit 7. He would then call out: 4-2-5-4-5. They can be called out in any order.

All you have to do is: mentally add together the digits called out. The sum in this case will be 20. Now add these to digits: 2 plus 0 equals 2. Now subtract this sum from 9. The answer is 7, the number the spectator chose to write down.

This is all you ever have to do, whatever numbers are chosen by the spectator: Subtract the final number from 9.

You will always be correct. Practise this on your calculator — fantastic.

Chapter Four

Mental Magic

If there is one kind of magic that has captured the most interest the last few years, it is mental magic.

Can someone predict what will happen in the future? Can a person read someone else's thoughts? Can you project a thought and have another person grasp it?

There is really no proof that these things can be done, or have been done. But it's still an interesting idea. So if you can seem to be doing some of these things during a magic performance it will certainly grab your audience's attention, and stimulate their imagination.

Just as there are magicians who specialize in doing coin tricks, there are those who specialize in mental effects. These people are called "mentalists", or "mentalist-magicians". I am one of these specialists, and I prefer to call myself a "mentalist-magician" because I don't want to pretend to have special powers that others do not have.

Mentalism is just another way of presenting magic. In order to make it really interesting you should be able to speak well, in order to make the tricks more convincing. By learning to use good wording and speaking well, you will be developing an ability that will be very useful all your life.

So, here we go with the mental stuff.

Ghostwriting

◆ What the audience sees:

Hand someone a small piece of white tissue paper, about 4 by 4 centimetres square. Ask her to hold it after making sure there is nothing written on it. Then say to your audience: "Would someone please think of the name of a famous television star? Now name that person."

If several names are called out, have the audience agree on one. Then ask the person holding the paper to bunch it up into a tiny pellet and hand it to you. Drop it into a cup and say: "Will everyone please concentrate on the chosen name. No talking please. The friendly spirit who does my magic will be listening to your thoughts."

After a few moments of silence, ask someone to pick up the pellet and open it. Written on the paper, in a shaky handwriting, will be the name of the selected TV star.

◆ Preparation ahead of time:

Cut out two identical pieces of paper from some wrapping tissue. Stick the edge of one to a small piece of stiff cardboard with a tiny bit of rubber cement. Place this into a pocket with a small pencil stub. The other paper you will hand out. Have a cup ready.

◆ How the trick is presented:

While everyone is concentrating on the name, have your hands in your pockets. Grasp the small pencil and write the chosen name on the paper in your pocket. The stiff cardboard will act as a backing to aid your writing.

Pull the paper away from the cardboard, crunch it up tightly like the other pellet and conceal it between your first two fingers. Reach out with the same hand to take the other pellet — and when you dip your hand down to the cup, simply drop the concealed pellet and retain the other one in your hand.

A little practice will show you how easy this is. Later, you can drop the blank pellet into your pocket while everyone is looking at the name which has appeared by magic on the paper!

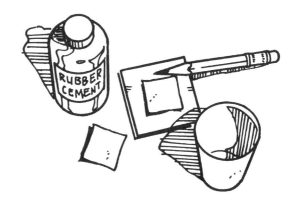

Knowing the News

◆ What the audience sees:

After you have finished reading your newspaper, tear out seven pieces from different pages, each piece roughly containing a separate story. Crumple each strip into a ball and lay out the seven balls on a tabletop. Pick up two balls, one in each hand, and say "Will someone point to one of these and I will throw it away." Afterwards, place the remaining ball on the table with the others. Now have a spectator pick up any two balls and you select one of these to be discarded. Then it's your turn to again pick up two.

Repeat this until only one ball is left on the table. Then say: "Just by chance, this is the last ball remaining. Will someone open it up, see what the story is about and I will try to read your mind." And that is exactly what you do.

◆ How the trick is presented:

When you are tearing out the different strips, concentrate on the headline of just one of them. You will then know what the story is about. After you crumple it into a ball, just remember where that particular ball is placed. Whenever you pick up two balls, always leave the memorized one on the table.

When the spectator picks them up, if one of them is the key ball, choose the other one for him to discard. So the key ball will always be the last one left.

Remember to pretend to be reading the spectator's mind when he or she is looking at the story. Just say a few general things about it. The headline will give you a good idea of its contents.

Partners

◆ What the audience sees:

On a table top, place a penny, a nickel, a dime, a quarter, a dollar bill, a $5 bill and a $10 bill. Tell the audience that your assistant has strange mind reading abilities. Send him or her out of the room.

Next, ask a spectator to point to any one of the items on the table. Then say: "Would someone please call the mind reader back into this room and ask her to name the item which was chosen. I will not speak to her at any time."

When your assistant returns, she will immediately approach the person who did the pointing and say: "I feel that you are the one who is guiding my thoughts. Now, will you please look right into my eyes and think of the item you were pointing to." After a few minutes, she will say "I think I am getting the message" and name the chosen item.

◆ Preparation ahead of time:

You and your assistant must devise a code with which you can give her signals. There are many ways you can do this. For example, if the spectators are seated in a row to your left, each can be assigned a number — next to you is 1, the next person is 2 — and so on. When your assistant enters the room, you can indicate with your fingers which number it is. For the coins and bills, you can have a different signal for each item: for example, touch your right elbow with your left hand, brush back your hair, pull your ear lobe, rub your right or left eye.

◆ How the trick is presented:

When your assistant enters the room after the item has been chosen, be sure to make your signals very carefully, so that they are not noticed by the audience. Just sit back and relax.

Your assistant, too, should take her time, not staring directly at you. Remember, you are not supposed to say a word. Don't draw any attention to yourself. All eyes will be on the mind reader.

Timed

◆ What the audience sees:
Ask someone who has a watch with a second hand to look at her watch and concentrate on the second hand. Say, "Believe it or not, I can tell time by my mental powers. Please select any number of seconds up to a minute. What have you selected?"

Suppose she calls out 30 seconds. You then say, "Alright, watch your second hand and time it when I call out 'START'."

You then call it out and, after a certain time, call out "STOP." The spectator will confirm that you have timed exactly 30 seconds.

You can then repeat this trick once or twice if you like.

◆ Preparation ahead of time:
In a way, you are telling the truth when you claim to be using your mental powers. You are really using your internal clock—your pulse. Before presenting the trick, measure your pulse at your wrist. Notice how many pulse beats you get for 15 seconds, for 30 seconds, for 45 and for 60.

Remember those figures. When the spectator announces a certain time, you'll know how many beats you should get. Any intervals between the measured ones are easy to estimate.

You may be off by a second or two. If you want to be more accurate, just ask the spectator to select 15, 30, 45, or 60 seconds.

◆ How the trick is presented:
When the timing begins, hold your hands behind your back, press your right thumb to your left wrist and count your pulse beats.

When you arrive at the appropriate number of beats for the selected time, you just call out "STOP." You'll be bang on.

There's an even better way of doing this. If you put your hand to the side of your forehead, and lightly press the tip of your middle finger to your temple, you'll find a pulse beat there.

This is a natural way of pretending to concentrate, by holding your hand to your forehead. Remember to be very serious and mysterious about this whole thing. After all, you're really supposed to be a magician. Play the part.

Dial-A-Trick

◆ What the audience sees:

Have someone shuffle a deck of cards and spread them out, face up on a table. Say "I would like someone to select a card, any card you wish, from the 52 you are looking at."

After this is done, say "You can change your mind and select a different card if you wish — this is a completely free choice."

When a card is decided upon (let us say it is the 6 of Spades), say "Now I'm going to telephone someone who has the strange power that she is able to see over the telephone. Please place the card face up near the phone."

Now you dial a number and when someone answers, you say "Is Laura there?" Then you hand the phone to one of your spectators, saying "I won't even speak to her, you might think I am giving her some information.

"Just ask her if she can name the card by looking at it over the telephone."

When the spectator does this, a voice will be heard saying "I can see the card but it isn't too clear. I seems to be the 6 of Clubs. No, no it's the 6 of Spades."

Your audience will be astounded.

◆ Preparation ahead of time:

The person you are calling will be a friend of yours. You will teach her a simple code so that she will know what card has been chosen. Firstly, each suit will have a different girl's name. For example, Spades will be Laura, Clubs will be Sandra, Hearts will be Rita and Diamonds Shirley.

In this way, when you call and ask for Laura, your friend instantly knows that the card is a Spade.

The code for the number is simple. When you call, let the phone ring six times, then hang up, saying that you have dialed wrongly. In this way, your friend knows the number of the card is a 6. Ring again and she will answer.

The Jack will be 11 rings, the Queen 12 and King 13. Just tell your audience that you think your friend is not home, hang up and dial again. Your friend will answer the second time.

Try this trick. It is a knockout!

Madame Zola

Here is another great telephone trick.

What the audience sees:

A spectator selects any card from a deck of cards and shows it to everyone in the room, including yourself. You then pick up the phone and call Madame Zola, the Mystic Mind Reader. When she answers, you let the person who chose the card speak to her. Madame Zola, through her mystical powers, tells this person the name of the card.

Preparation ahead of time:

Madame Zola is a friend of yours. You teach her a secret code.

How the trick is presented:

When your friend answers the phone you say, "Is Madame Zola in?" She immediately starts naming the four suits, "Diamonds, Clubs, Spades, Hearts." As soon as she names the suit of the chosen card, which you know, you interrupt by saying "Would you call her to the phone, please." Your friend now knows what the suit is.

She then starts calling out the numbers "Ace, two, three, four" etc. When she calls out the correct number, you can again interrupt by saying "Hello, Madame Zola, please hold the line" and give the phone to the spectator. Madame Zola now knows the exact card through the secret code.

But she doesn't just name the card. She makes it seem difficult by saying things like "I seem to see a red card, no, it's a black card" and then announces what the card is. Try this one — it's a super trick.

Colorful

◆ **What the audience sees:**
Toss 10 different-colored wax crayons onto a table and turn your back to the audience, with your hands behind your back. Say "I'd like someone to choose one crayon and place it in my hands." After this is done, tell the audience: "Would you please concentrate on the color of this crayon — I will try to read your minds." Keeping the crayon in your left hand, behind your back, bring forward your right hand and place it to your forehead as if you are deep in thought. "Ah yes — I can see the color now. It is blue." Whatever the color chosen, you will be correct. You can even repeat this trick immediately.

◆ **How the trick is presented:**
When the crayon is placed in your hands behind your back, turn around so that you are facing the audience again. Make sure that no one can see your hands, which are still behind your back. Hold the crayon in your left hand and dig one of your right hand fingernails into it so that some of the crayon remains under your fingernail. Just take a small amount. When you bring your right hand to your forehead, do it slowly. This will give you time to peek at your fingernail as your hand comes up.

There is the color of the crayon, nice and clear. After that, don't rush to name the color. Pretend you are reading the minds of the audience. If you repeat this little miracle, remember to use a different finger the second time. Colorful trick, isn't it?

That's Odd

◆ What the audience sees:

Place between 10 and 15 coins on the table. Spread them out. Turn your back to the table and ask a spectator to turn over any coin, any number of times.

Say, "You can keep turning the same coin or turn different coins. The only thing I will ask you is to say 'turn' each time you turn one over. When you're finished, push one coin aside, see if it's heads or tails up, then cover it with your hand."

After this is done, face the table, push the coins aside, look into the person's eyes and say, "I will now read your mind and tell you which side of the covered coin is facing up."

You do just that.

◆ How the trick is presented:

When you first place the coins on the table, do a quick mental count of how many heads, or tails, are showing. Let us say it's heads you choose to remember. Just remember is it's an odd or even number.

Let's say it's odd. Now, every time the spectator says "turn," just make a mental change to your memory of the heads. At the first "turn," say "even" to yourself. Then "odd" and so on.

Suppose you end up at "even." When you turn back, do a fast mental count of the heads. If there are an even number showing, then the hidden coin will be tails up. If an off number, it will be heads up.

That's all there is to it. But the basic idea is to make it seem like mind reading. So gaze into the person's eyes, ask her to concentrate and to think of the hidden coin. Then slowly reveal what you think it is.

Make it dramatic. Before you begin the eye-to-eye part, slowly push the coins aside — and under cover of that action, quickly do your mental count to find out even or odd.

That way, it won't be noticed that you are counting the coins.

Super Memory

What the audience sees:

Show two different hard-covered books. Hand one to a spectator, saying, "I'd like you to have this one because I've memorized every word in the book. I'll keep the other, because I haven't studied it yet."

Then ask someone to call out any page number. Suppose it is 110. Turn to that page in your book. Ask someone to call out a number from 1 to 20. Suppose it is 12. Say: "All right, I'll check the 12th line on this page." Then read out: "This line says 'He crossed the room as everyone watched him'."

Now say, "If you had asked me for the twelfth line on page 110 in your book, I wouldn't have had to look it up. That line would read..." and you call out certain words. Have the spectator check the book you "memorized," which he is holding, at the page number and line. You will be exactly right.

Preparation ahead of time:

You must get three books with dust jackets. Two are identical. The third is different. Remove the dust jacket from one of the identical books and replace it with the jacket from the third, different book. Set aside the third book. You will now be using two identical books but they will have different jackets, so your audience will think they are different books.

How the trick is presented:

Hand the spectator the book with the correct jacket on it. Everyone will think your book is different. When they name the page and line, you turn to it but don't read it aloud, because it's the same as in the book they have. Instead, you make up a line and read that. When you finish, concentrate hard on the actual line you read — and that's what you tell them they have in their book.

Just watch the expression on their faces when they check it out. then take back the book from them and put both books away. Then go on to your next trick.

The Sniffer

◆ What the audience sees:

Someone escorts you out of the room in which your audience is gathered. They blindfold you and return you to the room after the audience has decided on some small object in the room that you must locate. You must move around the room, touching various objects, until you pick up one particular item and say, "This object is transmitting magic vibrations which I can feel." Believe it or not, you have found the secret item.

◆ Preparation ahead of time:

You have a friend in the audience who acts as your secret assistant. Before you perform, you tell him what to do. You divide the room into four imaginary quarters. When you enter the quarter that contains the object, he is to make a sniffing sound with his nose. When you touch a large object which holds the secret item he is to sniff again. When you touch the secret object itself, he is to do a double sniff.

◆ How the trick is presented:

When you are led, blindfolded into the room where the audience is waiting, tell your escort, "Just lead me to the centre of the room." From that point, you will enter one of the quarters as you begin to move around. Listen for the first sniff. The audience will not notice it. Now you know which area to concentrate on. Continue, by touching large objects, and listening for the next sound clue. When you finally locate the secret object, make a big fuss about it. That's the way to get applause. It's a good idea to practice this with your friend beforehand, so you'll become quite good at it. Remember, the nose knows.

Mentalla

◆ What the audience sees:

Place a book, a pencil, an envelope and a pair of dice on a table. Ask someone to shake and roll the dice, saying: "Keep doing it until you wish to stop. Right there? OK. What is your number?"

If it's a 5, for example, say: "Turn to chapter five in this book. Look at the first few words and concentrate on them. Don't think of anything else. Don't say anything, just think of those words."

Now pick up the envelope, remove a slip of paper from inside of it and write something on the paper. Replace it in the envelope and seal it. Ask the person: "Now will you read those words out loud, so we all know what they are?"

After this is done, tear open the envelope, have someone remove the slip of paper and read out loud what you have written. You have evidently read the person's mind — the words on the paper are the same as those in the book.

◆ Preparation ahead of time:

Open the flap of the envelope. Print the number 2 inside the flap at the top, left, just under the gummed edge. Beside the number, print the first three words of chapter two. Below it, do the same for chapter three and right up to chapter 12. Place the blank slip of paper into the envelope. Close the flap but don't seal it.

◆ How the trick is presented:

The dice will always end up with a number from 2 to 12, so these are the only chapters that can be chosen. And you have the information. When you open the flap to remove the paper, just glance at your notes, see the words you need, write them on the paper, replace it and then seal the envelope. When you want to have the paper removed, tear off one end of the envelope and have someone remove the paper. If the spectator has concentrated on more than three words, it doesn't matter. The fact that you got the first three is quite enough. this is really a super trick! Try it and see.

Think-A-Card

◆ **What the audience sees:**
Spread a deck of cards face up on the table. Have a spectator select any four cards. Ask her to think of just one of them but not to name it out loud. Place the four cards in your pocket. Say "Think of your card," then take them out, one at a time. The last one you remove will be the thought-of card.

◆ **Preparation ahead of time:**
Place any three cards in your pocket.

◆ **How the trick is presented:**
Place the four selected cards in numerical order as you pick them up, so you can remember the order they're in. Put them in your pocket beside the three cards already there. Remove those three cards one at a time, placing them face down on the table so nobody knows they are not from the four selected cards. These four are still in your pocket but everyone thinks you have only one left. Now, ask the spectator to name her thought-of card. Take that particular card out of your pocket — the cards are in order so you know which one to pull out.

Show it face down like the others, then slowly turn it over. Abracadabra, you have read someone's mind.

It's Chinese To Me

 What the audience sees:
Have someone shuffle a deck of cards. Take it and place it face down on the table. Write something on a slip of paper, fold it and give it to the spectator, whom we'll call John. Write something on another paper and give it to another person, let us say Ann. Then give the cards to Ann and say, "Deal any number of cards on the table, face down, look at the last card you dealt [it will be on top], remember it and place these cards back on top of the deck. Then give the deck to John." Ask John to deal the same number of cards, one on top of the other and to look at and remember the last card. Then you place the cards he dealt back on the top of the deck. Ask him to read out loud the note you gave him. It will name the card he dealt last and remembered. Then ask Ann to read her note. This will amuse the audience because she can't. It's in Chinese. However, you will translate by naming the card it represents. And that will be the card she looked at and remembered.

◆ **How the trick is presented:**
When you take the deck after it has been shuffled, slide the top card aside slightly and peek at it. That's the card you write down on the note to John. On the second paper, draw something that looks like a couple of Chinese symbols. Now the trick works itself. All you have to do is, when you pick up the cards that John dealt, glimpse and remember the bottom card before you place the packet on the deck. That will be the card that Ann looked at and that's the card you name when you "translate" the Chinese characters. Try this trick by yourself — it works.

Chapter Five

Miscellaneous Magic

This chapter contains a hodgepodge of all kinds of magic. There's something for every taste.

Do you like to do magic with ropes? With string? With salt? With paper? With matches? With almost anything? It's in this chapter.

And remember, we stick to our basic rule: all the effects can be done with everyday objects, easy to obtain.

There's a trick with some grapes, and you can even eat them when you're done. There's a great trick where you magically produce a lemon. If you want to end up by eating it—alright, if that's your taste.

This being the last chapter, I think I should say a few words about "routining," which means the order in which you do your tricks.

If you are going to be with some friends, and plan to do a little show for them, have everything ready in your pockets or in a little container. Plan the order in which you are going to do the tricks.

When you do your performance it will seem to the audience that you are just doing a number of impromptu effects. But you yourself must be working with a definite plan. This will make the whole show run very smoothly. And, most important, keep it short. Don't go on and on.

The first rule of showbusiness: Always leave the audience wanting more!

The Vanishing Glass

◆ **What the audience sees:**
Wrap a piece of newspaper around a glass tumbler which is standing, open end down, on a table at which you are seated. The paper will take the shape of the tumbler. Place a coin on the table and cover it with the paper-covered glass which is still upside down. Say "I will cause the coin to vanish." Slap your hand down on the glass then pick it up (still paper-covered). The coin is still there. Cover it again. This time the paper is completely flattened down. The coin is still there, but *the glass has vanished.*

◆ **How the trick is presented:**
After the first slap-down you seem to have failed. Say something like "Oh my, something went wrong. May I try it just one more time?" At the same time lean back in your chair, bringing the paper-covered glass, which you had lifted to reveal the coin, beyond the edge of the table. While the spectator is listening to you and looking at the coin, loosen your grip on the glass. It will slip out of the paper and drop to your lap. You still retain your grip on the paper which will keep the shape of the glass. Everybody thinks the glass is still there. Place the paper form over the coin as you did before. Smack your hand down on it. Bang — no glass. A real surprise.

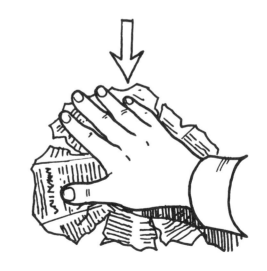

Moondust

◆ What the audience sees:
Show a small box containing Magic Moon Dust "made from rocks brought back from the moon." Have a spectator close her hand into a fist. Pour a little Moon Dust into your hand. Blow it into the air. Say, "Open your hand." There is the missing Moon Dust, in her own hand. Impossible, but true.

◆ Preparation ahead of time:
Put some cigarette ashes into a small container, like a pillbox. Lick the tip of the middle finger on your left hand, then dip it into the ashes. Quite a bit of the ash will cling to your finger. Bend it into the palm of your hand so the ash can't be seen.

◆ How the trick is presented:
Ask the spectator to extend her right hand, palm down. Grasp it with your left hand and say "Hold it a little lower" as you lower it. Then say, "Now close it into a fist."

As you say that, press your middle finger against her palm. The dirty work is now done. You have left some moon dust in her palm. Now show the little box, open it and talk about the moon rocks as you show the precious Moon Dust. Pour some in your hand and blow it in the air — it vanishes.

By this time, she has completely forgotten that you ever touched her hand. When she opens her fist and sees what it contains — wow, watch the expression on her face.

Penetrating Dice

◆ What the audience sees:

Roll a pair of dice on a table. Pick them up, one between the tip of the thumb and the forefinger of each hand. The left-hand die should have the 1 spot showing on top, when the forefinger and thumb are held horizontally. The right-hand die should be held to show the 2 spots on top.

Bring your hands together with the forefingers and thumbs pointing toward each other. Tap together the sides of the dice which are at the ends of your fingers and thumbs. After two taps, say "Watch carefully" as you again bring the dice together.

This time, push the dice together more forcefully. Suddenly, the dice will be seen to have penetrated each other. Your fingers will have been linked. The 1 spot is still showing in your left fingers, the two spots in your right fingers, an impossible penetration of two solid objects.

This trick can be repeated if you wish.

◆ How the trick is presented:

When you pick up the dice, hold the left one so that the 1 is up and the 2 is under the thumb. Hold the right die so that the 2 is up and the 6 is under the thumb.

When you bring your fingertips together to tap the dice, give the right-hand die a quarter turn towards you. Do this by turning your hand slightly, so that the 2 is facing you instead of facing up. Now your right-hand forefinger will be above the thumb instead of beside it. The left-hand position does not change.

Now, on the third tap, all you do is slide your fingers and thumbs along so that you switch grips on each die. You are now holding different dice in each hand, but they seem to be the same, because the 1 is still showing in your left fingers and the 2 in your right.

The dice appear to have penetrated each other and the sliding move will not be noticed. This might seem complicated to read but follow it with the dice in your hands. It's easy to do.

Knot Surprise

What the audience sees:

Hold a silk scarf by one end in your left hand. Lift the other end with your right hand and place it in your left hand so that the scarf now hangs down in a loop. Say, "I will now form a magic knot in this scarf — watch." Give the scarf a snap with your left hand and let one end drop down. No knot. "Oops," you say, "it didn't work. Let's try again." Repeat the same actions. Still nothing happens. Say, "Oh of course, I forgot to say the magic words. Let me try it one last time."

Then say your magic word: "Abracasomethingorother." Snap the scarf again and presto, there's a knot tied in the end that's hanging down.

Preparation ahead of time:

Use a scarf of silk or any other thin material. Tie a knot a few inches from one end of the scarf.

How the trick is presented:

When you hold the scarf in your left hand, be sure to have your hand around the knotted end, concealing the knot. When you snap it down the first two times, let the opposite end drop each time. Of course, nothing happens. After the second time, the spectators will think you have failed and won't be paying too close attention the third time. That's when you will be doing something different but it won't be noticed. When you bring the bottom end into your left hand, on top of the knotted end, shift your grip on the ends — so that when you snap the scarf, you hold onto the unknotted end and let the knotted end drop free. It looks exactly like the other moves but suddenly the knot appears from nowhere. It sounds simple but try it. The effect is very surprising.

Breakaway

◆ What the audience sees:
Remove a neatly folded handkerchief from your pocket and spread it out on a table. Place a few wooden matchsticks (or toothpicks) on the table and say "Will someone please take one match and lay it on the centre of the hanky." Then fold up the hanky with the match in its centre and hand it to someone, saying, "You can feel the match through the hanky. Now, hold the match with both hands and break it in half. You can break it into smaller pieces if you wish." Everyone will hear the match breaking inside the hanky. Take the handkerchief back, lay it on the table and slowly unfold it. There is the match, all in one piece, magically restored. Show your hands empty, pick up the hanky, show both sides of it, fold it neatly and place it back in your pocket. A miracle.

◆ Preparation ahead of time:
You must use a hanky that has a good-sized hem. Most men's linen handkerchiefs are made this way. At one corner of the hem, if there is no opening, cut a couple of stitches, push in a wooden match. It will not be noticed inside the hem.

◆ How the trick is presented:
When you fold the hanky after a match is placed in the centre, be sure to know where you are placing the corner with the hidden match. That is the part that you hand the spectator to hold and to break. Having just seen the one match, they are quite certain that is the one they are breaking. Before you unfold the hanky to reveal the one whole match, wave your hands over it and say a few magic words. After all, you *are* a magician. This is one of the first tricks I ever did, years ago — and no matter how many times I've performed it since, it still fools them.

Ribbonsation

◆ What the audience sees:
Show a tube made up of a rolled sheet of paper. Your audience sees it's empty, as they can see right through it. Wave your hand over it, say the magic words, and pull out a long strip of ribbon from "nothingness."

◆ Preparation ahead of time:
Roll an 8 by 11-inch sheet of typing paper into a tube with a diameter of about 1 1/2 inches. Scotch tape it to hold together. Roll a second sheet the same way, but a little tighter. Don't tape it. Slip it inside the first tube. You now have a double-walled tube. At one end tape the edges of both rolls together. When you look at that end you will not see the two layers because they are taped together. Separate the layers at the other end and push about two feet of ribbon down into the hidden space between the two sheets. Use gift-wrapping ribbon, about one-half inch wide, of a bright color. Just fold it in pleats and push it into the secret compartment with a pencil. You're all set to go.

◆ How the trick is presented:
Show the "empty" tube, always directing the taped end toward the spectators. The open end containing the ribbon points toward you. To the viewer, the tube appears completely empty and he has no reason to suspect otherwise. Now, make some magical gestures over the tube, use your favorite magic words and reach into the secret compartment with your thumb and forefinger. Slowly pull out the ribbon. Try to look surprised — this will amaze your audience even more.

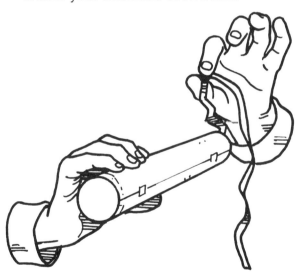

The Travelling Ring

◆ **What the audience sees:**
You hold a borrowed finger ring at the tip of your left hand thumb and forefinger. Borrow a handkerchief and drape it over your left hand, ring and all. Have someone place a rubber band around your left wrist, encircling the hanky. This will seal off your left hand with the ring inside the hanky. Have someone cover and rubber-band your right hand with another hanky in the same manner. Now, keeping your hands far apart, give them each a shake, saying "Go."

When the hankies are removed, the ring will be seen to have magically vanished from the left hand and to have appeared in the right.

◆ **How the trick is presented:**
When you drape the hanky over your left hand, that is the time to do the secret move. Hold the hanky by one edge in your right hand. Hold it on the far side of your left hand, between your hand and the audience, shielding your hand from the audience.

Draw the hanky back over the left hand towards yourself, in order to cover the hand. As you do so, clip the ring between your right-hand thumb and the hanky, pulling it away from the left thumb and forefinger tips.

As you complete pulling the hanky over your left hand, simply let the ring drop into your right palm and conceal it as you drop your hand to your side. Your right fist will be closed, with the ring inside it, when the hand is covered with the second hanky.

Be sure to act dramatically when you shake your hands back and forth before the hankies are removed. That's what makes it seem like real magic. The secret move will require a little practice, but it's well worth it.

This may seem like a difficult trick but a lot of things are tough when you first try them. Stick with it!

Bewildering Bracelet

◆ What the audience sees:

Hand a solid bracelet to a spectator, saying "Please examine this. Make sure there are no breaks or openings in this bracelet." Hand someone else a short piece of rope, asking "Would you please tie each end of this rope to each of my wrists and make several knots so that they're very secure." After this is done, take the bracelet back and turn around so that your back is to the audience. After a moment, turn around and show that the bracelet is now hanging from the rope between your wrists. The rope is still firmly fastened to each wrist. Apparently the bracelet has magically penetrated the rope. It's quite a surprise.

◆ Preparation ahead of time:

You will need two solid bracelets which are identical. You can buy plastic ones at Woolworth's or Kresge's which are perfect for this trick — and are good for other tricks, too.

Have a piece of rope or heavy string ready, about three feet long. Also, you must wear a long-sleeved jacket. Slide one of the bracelets up one arm under your jacket sleeve until it holds tight on your arm. It will not be seen.

◆ How the trick is presented:

After each end of the rope is tied securely to each wrist, take the second bracelet from the spectator. As soon as you turn your back to the audience, immediately place that bracelet into an inside jacket pocket. This, of course, will not be seen. Then slide the hidden bracelet down your arm and onto the rope. Do all this as quickly as you can, then turn back to the audience. It's magic.

Fruit Fun

◆ What the audience sees:

When it comes to dessert time at dinner, reach over to the fruit bowl, pluck several grapes from a bunch, place them on the table and ask someone to pick up a few and conceal them in his or her hand. Pick up a matchbook, tear out a match, light it and hold it under the hand holding the grapes.

Say, "The magic match will tell me how many grapes you're hiding." Then, blow out the match, look at it and call out the number. You will be correct. Then, show everyone the match. To their surprise, they will see the correct number etched on the burnt-out matchhead.

◆ Preparation ahead of time:

Take a matchbook and bend six matches forward. With a sharply pointed pencil, mark the head of each match with the numbers 1 to 6. Push back the matches to their original position. Have another matchbook in your pocket with one match torn out. You are all set.

◆ How the trick is presented:

When you reach for the grapes, be sure to tear off exactly six. When the spectator picks up a few simply deduct the amount remaning on the table, to know the number in her hand. When you tear out a match, just select the one with the proper number on it. After you blow out the flame, the number still remains visible, but spooky looking.

As soon as you tear out the match, drop the matchbook in your pocket. If someone asks to see it later, pull out the other one. It will look perfectly normal, with one match missing.

Restoration

◆ What the audience sees:

Show a piece of soft rope or thick string, about three feet in length. Fold it in half and hold the folded middle in your left fist with the doubled rope hanging down below your fist. With your right forefinger and thumb, pull a bit of the folded middle above your left fist so it can be seen. Hand someone a pair of scissors and have them cut right through the middle of the rope.

Your audience can now see two separate pieces of rope held vertically by your left hand. Take the scissors and cut away the small ends showing above your fist. Then, with your right hand, grab the end of one of the pieces hanging below the fist and pull the whole thing away with a flourish.

Believe it or not, the entire rope is restored to its original condition — one piece, three feet long.

◆ Preparation ahead of time:

Cut an extra piece of rope about five inches long. Fold it in half and hide it in your left fist with the folded middle toward your thumb. Make sure no one spots it.

◆ How the trick is presented:

After you place the folded long rope into your left fist and pretend to pull out the folded middle above your fist, you actually pull out the folded middle of the hidden small piece. It is that piece that is cut, not the long rope. It is then cut into small pieces to hide the evidence. These are allowed to drop to the floor. That's when you pull out the long piece, magically "restored." Impossible? Not for a magician.

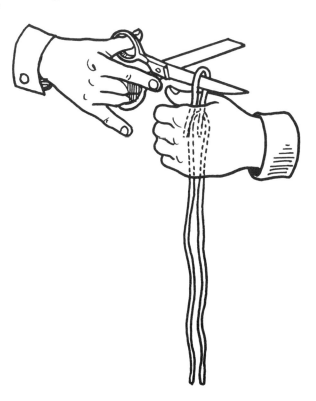

The Magic Twig

Here is some magic you can do out-doors.

◆ What the audience sees:

Pick up a small twig or stick from the ground, examing it and say, "Well, well, here's a magic memory stick. I haven't seen one of these in years."

Hand it to a friend, saying "Scratch your initials in the dirt with the tip of this memory stick." After he does that, ask him to erase the initials by scuffing them out with his shoe. Pick up some of the loose earth and rub it on your bare fore-arm. Then take the stick and tap your arm with it. Like magic, your friend's initials will appear on your arm. It looks really spooky.

"Ah," you say, "the magic memory stick strikes again!"

◆ Preparation ahead of time:

Get a small jar of transparent rubber cement such as you use for sticking paper together. With the attached brush print your friend's initials on your forearm. It will remain sticky but will not be seen.

◆ How the trick is presented:

Find a spot where there is some loose dirt and where some small sticks are lying around. When you rub the dirt on your arm, the whole arm will be covered. But when you tap it with the stick, most of the earth will fall off, except that which clings to the rubber cement.

It's quite a surprise when the initials are revealed! It's even better when there is a stranger in the audience. Try to find out his initials beforehand and use those initials. That's a double surprise.

To remove the rubber cement later on, simply rub it back and forth with your fingertips. It will peel right off.

The Rising Ring

◆ **What the audience sees:**

Remove a pencil from your pocket. Hold it at one end with the other end pointing up in front of you. Borrow a ring from someone and drop it over the top end of the pencil so that it encircles the pencil. The ring will drop to the bottom of the pencil into your fingers. Now say, "I will now cause the ring to move, using the power of my mind. Rise, ring, rise."

Slowly the ring rises to the top of the pencil until it jumps right off. Very spooky.

◆ **Preparation ahead of time:**

Get a long, unused pencil — the kind without an eraser. Cut a small slot across one end, about a quarter-inch deep. Take a piece of fine black thread about 15 inches long and knot one end. Drop that end into the slot on the pencil and pull it tight so the knot catches and fastens the thread to the pencil. Tie the other end of the thread to a lower button on your shirt or blouse. Place the pencil in one of your pockets.

◆ **How the trick is presented:**

When you take out the pencil, hold it by the end without the slot, and keep it fairly close to your chest. The thread should not be noticeable. When the ring is dropped over the pencil and falls to the bottom, the thread will also be enclosed by the ring. To make the ring rise, all you must do is slowly move the pencil away from you. The tightening thread will do the job.

You can make the ring stop, or go up or down by moving the pencil back and forth. But always move it slowly.

Experiment ahead of time so that you get the correct length of thread to do this properly. This is what we call visual magic — it looks great.

The Vanishing Pen

◆ What the audience sees:

Show a ballpoint pen. Remove the cap from it and show that the pen writes. Then hand out the pen to be examined. Say, "You'll notice it seems to be solid. But if I say the magic word, it will dissolve into nothingness."

Then pull up your sleeves, take back the pen, wrap both hands around it and shout: "Presto! Go!" Open your hands. The pen will have completely vanished!

◆ Preparation ahead of time:

You must use one of those inexpensive pens that has a removable cap on it — one that has a pocket clip on it. Get a piece of black cord elastic and cut off a piece about 30 centimetres long. If you can't find that, just take several rubber bands, cut them and tie them together.

Tie one end of the elastic to the clip of the pen and fasten a safety pin to the other end.

You must wear a jacket. Fasten the pin to the inside back of the jacket, just below the collar. Make sure that when the pen hangs down, it doesn't show below the bottom of the jacket. If so, shorten the elastic.

◆ How the trick is presented:

Have the pen ready in your right hand before you begin. This will stretch the elastic, of course. Remove the cap to show the pen and to hand it around. You will be holding on to the cap, with the elastic concealed behind your right arm.

Keep your right side to the audience to help this concealment.

When the pen is returned to you, insert it back into the cap and make sure it's tightly fastened.

When you make the pen vanish, move your hands quickly up and down, as you release your grip on the pen. This will hide any possible glimpse of the pen as it flies under your jacket.

Remember — make a big production out of waving your hands and shouting out the "magic word." Try this in front of a mirror while you practise. You'll see that you will fool yourself.

Colorchange

What the audience sees:

Show a red pencil to your audience, holding it in your left hand. In your right hand is a small, yellow scarf — or one that has some yellow coloring in it. Say, "I will now attempt to magically transfer the color of this scarf to the pencil." After showing that the scarf is not concealing anything, place it around the pencil and rub it up and down a few times. Whip away the scarf and, presto, the red pencil has turned yellow. It can be examined and found to be perfectly normal.

Preparation ahead of time:

Find a piece of red-colored paper. Cut it to the correct size to fit snugly around a yellow pencil. Fasten it with a thin piece of transparent sticky tape. Make it snug but not too tight, so that you can slip it off easily. Do a neat job and it will look like an ordinary red pencil.

How the trick is presented:

As you stroke the pencil up and down with the scarf — keeping it covered at the same time — simply slip off the red paper on the last stroke of your scarf. It will be concealed by the scarf. Crumple it up inside the scarf as you squeeze it in your right hand and casually place the scarf, with the paper, in your pocket as the audience is concentrating its attention on the pencil which has suddenly changed color. The evidence is now concealed and the audience is astounded.

Shirtless

Here's a trick that has amazed audiences for years. It is really so simple but very entertaining. Now the secret is yours.

What the audience sees:

You ask a male member of your audience to step forward. he is wearing a long-sleeved shirt with a jacket. You reach for the back of his shirt collar, grab it and slowly pull upwards. The entire shirt is pulled right out of his jacket.

Preparation ahead of time:

You must have a good-natured guy who will agree to be your assistant. Before the performance, in private, of course, have him remove his jacket and his shirt. Then put the shirt on him in the following manner: Drape it over his shoulders and on his back. Fasten the top two buttons in front of him in the normal manner. It's like a cape — his arms do not go in the sleeves. Now just button the sleeve cuffs around his wrists. Now when you put the jacket on him and button it, you can see the buttoned cuffs protruding from the jacket sleeves and the visible part of the shirt is buttoned in front.

How the trick is presented:

Simply unbutton the shirt cuffs and the top front of the shirt. Don't tell the audience what is about to happen. Just grab the collar at the back and say, "I will now attempt the impossible." Then pull.

Fingerprints

◆ What the audience sees:
Lay out 10 paper clips in a row on a table, making sure they are in a vertical position, parallel to each other. Ask a spectator to move as many clips as he or she wishes, one at a time, from the right end to the front of the left end of the row, so that the one that was first, ends up being somewhere in the middle. Be sure you turn your back first.

After this is done, turn back and touch your fingertips to the spectator's fingertips, saying "Now that I've picked up your fingerprints, I can easily find out how many clips you have moved."

Now touch your fingers to the paper clips, and after touching each one of them, name the number that were moved. You can repeat this trick. You will always be right.

◆ Preparation ahead of time:
You will notice that a paper clip has one open end on the outside. When you lay the clips out, make sure that all of them have their open ends on the left side. The last clip on the right should be laid down with its open end on the right side. This one is called the key clip. You are now ready to go.

◆ How the trick is presented:
When you turn your back, after the clips have been moved, simply notice where the key clip is located. Just add that clip to the ones to the left of it and you have the magic number.

The first clip to be moved will always be the key clip so you can see how easily it works. The business with the fingertips is important because it adds showmanship, makes the trick more entertaining and deflects the spectators' attention from the method being used.

A Nutty Trick

◆ What the audience sees:

Roll a paper napkin into a ball and place a cardboard party horn over it on a table. Then lift the horn and put the ball of paper in your pocket. Replace the horn on the table. Say, "Watch the invisible ball" as you point to your pocket and the table. Lift the horn—the ball is back under it. Place the ball back in your pocket and the horn back on the table. Say, "Let's try again" and lift the horn. Now there's a walnut under the horn!

◆ Preparation ahead of time:

Roll a napkin ball tightly into the horn. Have another one rolled up on the table. Place a small walnut in your right hand pocket.

◆ How it's done:

After the horn is first lifted to reveal the ball of paper, replace it with a sharp tap on the table, dislodging the hidden ball, which will drop to the table under the horn. When revealed, everyone will think it's the one in your pocket. Now remove it with your right hand, place it in your pocket and bring out the walnut hidden behind the bent fingers of your right-hand. Place your right-hand fingers around the horn with your thumb at the rear. Lift the horn to show there's nothing under it. As you replace it, drop the nut under it. Practise this. It's quite a surprise when they see the nut!

Isn't that nutty?

An Eye-Popper

You must wear a jacket to perform this little miracle.

◆ What the audience sees:

Have a cup containing about 20 grains of unpopped popcorn in it. Reach in with your right hand and remove several grains. Place them into your left fist. Have someone light a match and hold it about a foot below your left fist — not too close. Say, "Aha, I think they're just about popped by now." Open your hand. A bunch of white popcorn will pop out. Then say, "Now watch them disappear" and eat them.

◆ Preparation ahead of time:

Thread a long needle with a short piece of thread through the lining of your jacket at the rear, on the left side over your hip — just a few stitches are necessary. The thread should be short so that the needle hangs down just above the bottom of the jacket and cannot be seen. Push several pieces of popped popcorn onto the needle. Have a cup of unpopped grains on a table.

◆ How the trick is presented:

Reach into the cup with your right hand and grab several grains between your thumb and fingertips. As you pretend to pick them up, release them and close your hand. It looks as if you're holding some in your hand. As you do this, stand with your right side to the audience. At the same time, reach back under your jacket with your left hand and slip the popcorn off the needle hanging there. Close your hand to conceal the popcorn. Practise this: It's easy. Now, hold your left fist in front of you with the thumb and forefinger on top. Pretend to push the unseen grains from your right hand into the top of your left fist. Show your right hand empty. Then open your left hand...Magic!

Bang

What the audience sees:

Show an inflated blue balloon. Take a straight pin and stick it into the balloon. There will be a bang, but instead of disintegrating, the balloon will change color from blue to yellow. Again take the pin and plunge it into the balloon, saying, "With my magic touch the balloon will not burst" — and that's exactly what will happen. The pin can be seen sticking halfway into the balloon, which remains intact. Now, remove the pin and hand it to a spectator, saying "Now you try it." When the spectator punctures the balloon, it will burst.

Preparation ahead of time:

Place a yellow balloon inside a blue balloon with the open end of the yellow one projecting slightly. Blow up the yellow balloon — the blue one will inflate around it on the outside. Tie up both ends. Stick a small piece of transparent tape on one of your fingers where it will not be noticed. You're now ready to go.

How the trick is presented:

When you stick the pin into the blue balloon, be sure you don't make contact with the yellow one inside. The blue one will burst, revealing the yellow one. The transformation is quite surprising. Everyone will think the trick is over. Take advantage of their lack of attention to secretly press the sticky tape onto the balloon on the side facing yourself. When you stick the pin into the yellow balloon, make sure you push it through the tape. The balloon will not break — but it will when someone pushes the pin into any other part of the surface.

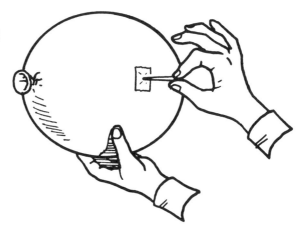

Salt Surprise

This is a good trick when you're at the table having dinner.

◆ What the audience sees:

Hand someone a paper napkin. Ask them to open it, examine it and return it to you. Take it in your left hand and drape it over your right hand. Then lift it by the centre with your left hand, with the edges hanging down. Now, with your right hand, twist the corners together and hold them, releasing the centre from your left hand. The napkin will hang down from your right hand like a little bag. Place a dish under the napkin as you hold it in the air. As you say "Would someone like some salt on their food?" use your left hand thumb and index finger to pinch a tiny tear in the bottom of the bag. A steady stream of salt will come pouring out.

◆ Preparation ahead of time:

Tear a small piece from a matching napkin and pour some salt into it. Gather the corners to form a tight little bag packed with salt. A little experimenting will guide you as to the size of the paper and the amount of salt. Conceal this little bag in your right hand which stays in your lap.

◆ How the trick is presented:

When you lift the napkin by the centre from your right hand, grasp the concealed bag of salt and lift it away under the napkin. When you form the napkin bag and hold it upside down in your right hand, the salt bag lies at the bottom of the larger napkin bag. Now, when you tear the paper, you will tear through the salt bag at the same time. Out pours the salt. After all the salt has descended, tear the napkin into pieces. The extra small piece will blend with the others. Your secret is safe!

Lemon-Ade

Here's a trick that looks like real magic.

◆ What the audience sees:

Hold a large handkerchief in front of you by two adjacent corners, with the hanky hanging down. Show both sides of it — nothing there. Your hands are seen to be empty. Release the left side and, with your left hand, pick up the hanky by the centre. Drape it over your right hand. Then whip away the hanky, revealing a lemon in your right hand. It will be quite a surprise to your audience.

◆ Preparation ahead of time:

Conceal a small lemon under your left armpit. Hold your arm close to your side and the lemon will not fall. Check in front of a mirror. Use a large linen hanky or square scarf which you cannot see through.

◆ How the trick is presented:

The tricky move is when you show both sides of the hanky. Holding the corners, bring the left hand to the right and the right hand behind it to the left. This will bring your right hand directly under your left armpit. Let the lemon drop into your right hand. When you straighten out the hanky, the lemon in your right hand is concealed behind the hanky. Now, when you pick up the centre of the hanky, grab the lemon underneath it and when you drape the hanky over your right hand, simply place the lemon on your right palm. When you whip away the hanky, presto, there's the lemon.

Practise these moves well, otherwise the lemon trick will go sour.